THE CHRISTMAS FOUNDATION; BEGINNING OF A NEW COSMIC AGE

RUDOLF GROSSE

Published in the original German by the School of Spiritual Science, Goetheanum, Dornach, Switzerland

For members of the General Anthroposophical Society

Authorized English translation of "Die Weihnachtstagung als Zeitenwende" © 1976 Philosophisch-Anthroposophischer Verlag, Goetheanum, Dornach

English translation by Johanna Collis

Cover design: Werner Kehlert, Van James

Contents

List of Illustrations

Preface to the Second German Edition

A second Impression of the book *Die Weihnachtstagung als Zeitenwende* has become necessary after only six months. This introduction to the spiritual and historical conditions prevailing at the re-founding of the General Anthroposophical Society has meanwhile been read in many study groups, often together with the quoted lectures by Rudolf Steiner, in the endeavour to achieve a deeper understanding of the Christmas Conference.

The author's main purpose was to learn to see Rudolf Steiner within the overall process of world history and so come to recognize his spiritual mission. Just as was the case at Christmas 1923, enthusiasm and new impulses will be born out of encountering and experiencing the nature of the Christmas Conference.

Rudolf Grosse

June 1977

Understanding the Christmas Conference

At the Christmas Conference in 1923, Rudolf Steiner formed the esoteric Vorstand of the Anthroposophical Society and himself took on the role of President. Since then this Christmas Conference has been the focal point of interest for the members of the Society. The processes and consequent changes were experienced as a re-founding of the Society and were seen by the members as an expression of a lofty spiritual event.

Both in personal study and in shared discussion during group meetings the theme of the Christmas Conference took members far beyond the bounds of a mere giving and receiving of information. As the years went by, however, it was found that there existed a certain limit to comprehension that was not easily overstepped. Reports by those who had participated in the Conference were borne by a warmth of enthusiasm which directly affected the listeners. Yet when concrete and clearly grasped concepts were sought it seemed that these lay outside the limits of what could be formulated. And just because of this, people desired to know more.

In 1944, twenty-one years after the Christmas Conference, Marie Steiner made the reports and minutes of the daily proceedings generally accessible for the first time, thus abundantly satisfying this desire. Everyone who had an opportunity during those wartime days sought to obtain a copy of her publication.[1] Its contents aroused a burning, undying interest in the event of the Society's founding. Rudolf Steiner depicted the association of the anthroposophists in its full nature and being in a way that allowed those present, and later the reader, to see in spirit the archetypal image of the Society. Day by day Rudolf Steiner spoke words one longed to learn by heart. Often in later years study groups, frequently consisting of young, earnestly striving members, also at youth conferences at the Goetheanum, sought to hear of the exact sequence of events from an older member who had actually been present at the Christmas Conference. Sometimes people felt as though they had been transported into the far distant past to the time when in just such a manner the supreme event of the Turning Point Of Time was reported from person to person by those who had been present. Thus it was indeed an event whenever a founder member of the Vorstand spoke to a gathering. Quite soon the mood of the Christmas Conference pervaded the room and one knew: It lives on!

Whether reading and studying or hearing reports of this kind, it was possible to build up a picture of what Rudolf Steiner had endeavoured to form as a community of human beings with the will to be guided solely by raising their eyes to the spirit. We read the report on the Conference which he wrote in his *Letters to Members* on 13 January 1924 and impressed the following sentences on our minds:

"To give the Anthroposophical Society the form most suitable for the development of the Anthroposophical Movement: this was the purpose of the Christmas Gathering which has just come to an end. A society of this kind can have no abstract rules or statutes. Its real basis is already given in all that insight into the spiritual world which is Anthroposophy. In this a large number of men and women today already find an impulse which they feel is worthy of their spiritual striving. The union in a society with others of a like mind is what their souls require. For in mutual give and take in spiritual matters, human life unfolds its truest essence. It lies in the nature of the case that those who would make Anthroposophy an integral part of their life should wish for a society through which to foster it."[2]

On 15 January 1924 Rudolf Steiner gave a lecture to members in which every sentence adds to our comprehension of what really took place during the Christmas Conference: "What happened here at Christmas must be understood as something which is not nearly finished, something which will not be brought to a close for a long time; it must be understood that the very least of what occurred at Christmas can be counted as concluded; rather we must realize that content must continue to flow into this Christmas Conference through whatever further takes place in the Anthroposophical Society."[3]

Then followed momentous words whose meaning has given rise to untold thoughts and conversations: "If you think back to this Christmas Conference you will realize that something was present there which came out of the spiritual world itself. The attempt was made to break with everything that might have smacked of the traditional way of running society affairs so that the spirit could shine through every single action that was carried out. But the spirit does have . . . its own laws. The spirit has other laws than those which hold sway in the physical world. If this Christmas Conference is treated as other conferences have so easily been treated in the past, then it will gradually evaporate, it will lose its content; and if this happens it would have been better if we had never gathered together in the first place. It is characteristic of the spirit that it disappears if it is not held fast. Of course it does not disappear in the cosmos but it departs from the place where it is no longer cultivated. It seeks out other places for itself in the cosmos instead. And for something like our Christmas Conference one does not depend, of course, on what happens within the earth realm."[2]

The passages quoted give an indication of the degree of inner understanding that would have to be developed in order to find the background of what "came out of the spiritual world itself". Every expression called for the unfolding of a deep spiritual intimacy with meanings that at first seemed utterly impenetrable. Maybe a further step is to realize the significance of the fact that so much connected with the Christmas Conference must remain enigmatic. The solution of life's riddles is linked to a person's inner maturity and this in turn is tied up with the development of the spiritual man. Paths into spiritual understanding are not open to the intellect alone. They must be sought in patience. Today we know, especially with regard to the Christmas Conference, just how much time it takes.

On the last day of the Christmas Conference, 1 January 1924, Rudolf Steiner once again spoke the *Foundation Stone Verses* he had spoken at the beginning, on 25 December 1923, verses which were intended to breathe new life into the ancient mystery summons "O Man, know thyself". A grand and solemn silence, deeply affecting, had pervaded the hall as it did on every subsequent morning over the next seven days. In the opening session of the Conference Rudolf Steiner had made a request: "May I please beg that we all endeavour to maintain the utmost solemnity of mood throughout this gathering".[1] The members complied. During these seven days, in as many stages, borne inwardly by the Foundation Stone Verses, they experienced in the ever changing rhythms of these verses, newly combined each day, something that later could only be described as participation in an act of spiritual creation. It was immeasurably great and there was no expression with which this daily process could have been described. All that could be said was that something new had been encountered in the spirit. The words spoken by Rudolf Steiner at the end of the Conference were borne by an infinity of spirit:

"To this end we have immersed ourselves in the words with which I began a week ago, — with which I will now close our Christmas Meeting. It shall have been for us a true "initiation night", a festival of initiation to inaugurate not just the beginning of a new year but the beginning of a Cosmic Turning Point Of Time. To this we will dedicate ourselves, in faithful cultivation of the spiritual life."[1]

Finally into the initiation mood of all those gathered there he uttered the words of summons to the soul:

"Soul of Man!
Thou livest in the limbs
Which bear thee through the World of Space
Into the ocean-being of the Spirit!
Practise Spirit-Recollection
In depths of Soul,
Where in the power sublime
Of World-Creator-Being
Thine own I
Comes to full being
In the I of God;

Rudolf Steiner

And thou wilt truly live
In Human-Cosmic-Being . . ."

In this last address Rudolf Steiner used words which made a deep impression through their most unusual sequence:

"Welten-Zeitenwende-Anfang"

"Beginning (of a) Cosmic Turning Point Of Time".

This phrase, coined by Rudolf Steiner, is like the spiritual seal impressed upon the Christmas Conference. This combination "Cosmic — Turning Point Of Time — Beginning" meets us like a great riddle. The last word, *beginning,* speaks to us most directly. Clearly and simply it states that we are faced with something new, something that has nothing whatsoever to do with the past. This Beginning raises up our entire being; in our soul, forces stir which desire to be free of the burden of the past. The Christmas Conference leaves the past behind, as an end, a conclusion, an abyss which is like a world fact. And beyond the abyss stands the Christmas Conference which itself is the Beginning of something that is new. For this New Unknown it is a light or indeed a star. Rudolf Steiner speaks impressively of this "Christmas star" which is there to light us on our way:

"Thus, my dear friends, carry out into the world your warm hearts, within which you have planted the Foundation Stone of the Anthroposophical Society. Carry your warm hearts into the world, to work there with strength and healing. And help will come to you, that your heads may be enlightened to direct with single purpose what you have here resolved. We make this resolution now with all our strength. And we shall see: if we prove worthy of it, a *good star* will prevail over what is here willed. Follow this good star, my dear friends, and we shall see whither the Gods will guide us by its light."

And then he turns directly to this light:

"O Light-Divine,
Christos-Sun,
Warm Thou
Our hearts
Enlighten Thou
Our heads!"

In connection with the image of the Christmas star and its light may be found an inconspicuous little phrase which in reality, however, is like a spiritual kernel containing and pointing towards some element of the secret of the Christmas Conference. It occurs in the farewell passage quoted above. Let us focus our attention on it:

"If we prove worthy of it, a good star will prevail over *what is here willed.*"

This phrase points to the germ of a spiritual future. *Something was willed* during the event of the Christmas Conference. In the face of this spiritual willing, human beings are required to develop and increase in dignity, for a good star is waiting to pour forth its light upon it:

Follow this good star!

It is spiritually correct to call these few farewell sentences which concluded the Christmas Conference an impressive Imagination of the star that will shine and lead us if we develop higher forces which enable us to rise up in *dignity*. Then "we shall see whither the Gods will guide us by its light".

Rudolf Steiner was making a perfectly concrete statement with the utmost seriousness when he said that the *beginning* would depend on the new *dignity* and earnestness, an earnestness encompassing all mankind. In the present age of inner independence, which is fitting for this culture epoch, we are surrounded by freedom, and also bear it within us as an effective force. Therefore this new beginning was given into the hands and into the responsibility of people, of members of the Anthroposophical Society which had been formed in this way. We realize how immeasurably great this responsibility is because the word *Beginning* does not stand alone. The beginning is seen in relation to the *Turning Point Of Time.* What kind of spirit is this who turns his gaze towards us from the Turning Point Of Time? He is the One with whom everything that was willed during the Christmas Conference must reckon, who was the foundation on which to build:

"At the Turning Point of Time
The Cosmic-Spirit-Light entered
The stream of earthly Evolution;
Darkness of Night
Had ceased to reign:
Day-radiant Light
Shone in the souls of men."

This happened 2000 years ago, when the Light-Divine, the Christos-Sun united himself with the earth. And now the message of the *Turning Point Of Time* is linked to the Christmas Conference itself. What did actually happen during the Christmas Conference? What is happening spiritually when during the Christmas Conference the Christos-Sun once again brings about the Beginning of the Turning Point Of Time? What turning point of time must this be, when just such a turning point has happened once before? When all is said and done, is perhaps the *Christmas Conference 1923* a point on an orbit of mankind that has become due once again in the cosmic-earthly sun place? If this is so — since this is the reality of the spiritual relation between earth and sun — then we can indeed speak of nothing other than a

Beginning of a Cosmic Turning Point Of Time

just as Rudolf Steiner did. These questions must be asked, as well as others later, in order to penetrate the silence that surrounds the Christmas Conference like an actual Mystery, in order to bring about the revelation of that which has not been spoken.

That this is in fact so, may be deduced from accounts given by Rudolf Steiner after the Christmas Conference, often with startling emphasis. Was it his purpose in a gentle way to raise into the light of individual experience the magnitude of the destiny that could be revealed to men through the working of the spirit of the Christmas Conference? Did he want all this to be imprinted unforgettably in the higher consciousness of all those whose privilege it was to come within the radius irradiated by the Christmas Conference, so that as a spiritual experience it might become a leading spirit light even after the conclusion of their paths on earth?

These questions pose us the task of seeking understanding. Let us set out on our quest by remembering the first *Turning Point Of Time.* What took place then, when the Christos-Sun entered into the darkness of night? Who at that Turning Point Of Time was able to perceive and experience the event? Was it not for the consciousness of mankind a process that ran its course in total imperceptibility, in utter secrecy, so that nothing penetrated the souls of that time? Should this star, whose purpose it is to shine and guide, pass once more unnoticed because there are still no eyes able to behold it? At that time the souls of men were so imprisoned by the sense-perceptible world and so bound to their bodies that the Christ Event did pass them by unnoticed. This must not happen again. We see one single human being, John the Baptist, who at that Turning Point Of Time did everything to shake his fellow men out of their state of soul, so that they might change their minds. Many allowed themselves to be baptised in order to become wakeful and perceptive in spirit; for one who was baptised experienced the whole of his life up to that moment and simultaneously also the spiritual world, thus coming to realize that in the spiritual world lives the "I" out of whom he has been born.

An observer of mankind cannot but be supremely distressed by what he perceives with hindsight to have been the condition of human beings at the beginning of the Christian era: The Central Event was prepared over thousands of years, so that the coming of Christ had to ensue out of the highest Spirit Being's decision for sacrifice; and yet mankind was not prepared, being inwardly blind and unable to create an organ with which this advent might be perceived. But this is not all. Anyone perceiving with spiritual eyes the spiritual constellation of mankind round about the end of the last century could not fail to experience a similar distress. This is best expressed in Rudolf Steiner's own words: "I had in mind at that time that the turn of the century would have to bring a new spiritual light for mankind. It seemed to me that the isolation of human thinking and willing from the spirit had reached a climax. A turnabout in the evolutionary progress of mankind seemed to me a necessity."[3]

In the distant past, John the Baptist, only a short time before the Baptism in the Jordan, had succeeded with a mighty and inspiring declaration in awakening the souls of men to the coming Turning Point Of Time. Rudolf Steiner worked in a different way. Out of his understanding of the development of mankind he knew that in the year 1899 a most important spiritual turning point in time would occur. The "age of spiritual light" was about to dawn, replacing the age of darkness, the Kali Yuga that had held sway for 5000 years. From then on, new spiritual capacities were to awaken in man. But a path would have to be prepared for these. Souls could only be released from the spiritual darkness linked with materialistic, natural scientific schooling if they could be given new spiritual concepts. It was just in this realm that men would have to change their mind, but a powerful and extremely intensive spiritual education would be necessary. For 30 years Rudolf Steiner worked at this task, from 1894 till his death in 1925.

In broad outline his *education of mankind* may be found in the books he published round about the turn of the century. A study of their titles and contents pages is enough to reveal his method. For example:

The Philosophy of Freedom":[4] a method of achieving body-free thinking;

Occult Science:[5] an understanding of evolution from the spiritual viewpoint, and also an expansion of consciousness in order to advance from indeterminate *forces* to the concrete working of spiritual *beings*.

Those who diligently study these descriptions are paving the way to an understanding of the reality of universal and human evolution.

Add to these *The Riddles of Philosophy*[6] and *Fundamentals of Therapy*[7] and you have before you the spirit structure of a universal body of knowledge founded on a definition of the universe, a conception of the world and a knowledge of man such as no single human being has ever accomplished. Having penetrated so deeply into the spiritual foundations and the development laws of evolution, Rudolf Steiner also succeeded in the task of founding a *Free High School for Spiritual Science*. The increasing assembly of students gathering at this High School, the Goetheanum, were trained to see and understand the being of *man* in a new way. Yet Rudolf Steiner never gave knowledge on its own. As in olden times, it was always linked with the development of an individual's being towards the higher man within him. The ancient Mystery words "O Man, know thyself" became once more the focal point of a spiritual, esoteric training. Two passages formed the core of this teaching: "The human being has the power to perfect himself, and with time to transform himself completely. For every human being bears within him besides his everyday personality a higher man." And on this path the golden rule applies: "For every one step that you take in the pursuit of higher knowledge, take three steps in the perfection of your own character."[8]

This is no more than an intimation of how within 30 years a new path of knowledge and development was travelled, a path evolving entirely out of the element of the *age of light* and demanding the inmost active soul forces of the human being.

In fulfilling his task, Rudolf Steiner took little notice of two factors: the objections of a civilization and of sciences founded on the thinking of a crumbling world in the age of darkness; and the opposition, the undermining influence arising out of unpurified soul forces unable to cope with their own unstable and contrary nature. In contrast, he was adamant in tackling the errors of thought, the superficiality of thought and the inconsistency of thought of some scientists and cultural personalities. Thus he taught people to be alert in their judgment, proving by such examples the disintegration of education and science. The truth of spiritual research was to be a healing force in this chaos of darkness, illusion and weakness.

If souls are to accept a new spiritual life of the kind being brought into the world by Anthroposophy, they will need to acquire two faculties: understanding and lack of prejudice. We must be prepared to overcome the narrow-mindedness and obstinacy inherent in standing on a point of view. An attitude of mind thoroughly schooled, in the philosophical sense of the word, is necessary, for with a sufficiently broad horizon this can win through to a clear understanding of how very much everything new must differ from all that is old and familiar; and how important it is to be inwardly independent in gaining familiarity with the new thoughts. Rudolf Steiner pointed many times to the methods of a spiritual seeker. It is necessary to investigate a fact or a research result from as many points of view as possible, never one alone, subsequently letting the varied, not to say contradictory, points bear each other out. This method can lead eventually to true spiritual maturity and nimbleness of mind.

Laying the Foundation Stone of the First Goetheanum

During the whole of his life Rudolf Steiner was constantly occupied with a certain direction of spiritual research. This concerned the questions of the being of Christ, His divine nature, His incarnation in Jesus of Nazareth at the Baptism in the Jordan, and the Mystery of His death. In the *Letters to the Members* Rudolf Steiner made every effort to throw light on the Mystery of Golgotha and the teachings of the Risen One in order to show how at the moment of dying the nature of death was spiritually overcome and transformed into true life by the Christ Force. He placed great importance on showing that through the Resurrection, which he called the *Mystery of Golgotha,* the whole historical process of mankind was given a new direction. In consequence, the biography of each single human being will increasingly be transformed from within if the resurrection forces of the Christ Impulse move his soul.

A life lived at the time of Christ bore certain characteristic qualities in the way the will and the personality, still so strongly permeated by luciferic elements, passed from birth to death. In post-Christian centuries, when inner qualities, through which a man might find himself, could be developed, something that had been impossible previously, the characteristic qualities of life were quite different. The capacity to develop strong forces from the soul, with which to meet the external world and destiny unbendingly and with assurance, also has something to do with this. Man can now achieve qualities of inward humanity which were quite unthinkable in former times. This light of resurrection, this human kindness and warmth will entirely transform, for instance, what we call medicine and education. The dominance of analytical thinking and of a purely scientific style of handling the riddles of existence can no longer be maintained.

If the social life of mankind is to become fruitful once more, the reality of the Christ Being will have to become the focal point of human existence. It is therefore necessary to concern ourselves with the significance of Jesus of Nazareth. Much may be read about Him in the lectures of Rudolf Steiner. He speaks about Him in a very special way in the *Gospel of Knowledge*, the so-called *Fifth Gospel*. The revelations he made out of his study of the Akashic Record should concern us in a particularly intimate way if we wish to study the Christmas Conference. This is because the laying of the Foundation Stone of the first Goetheanum, which took place on 20 September 1913, is linked with his research about the Fifth Gospel. This link was made clear in the following words spoken by Rudolf Steiner at the laying of the Foundation Stone:[9]

"As a first revelation of the Fifth Gospel there shall even now sound forth the macrocosmic counter-image of the microcosmic Prayer that was once proclaimed from east to west. So let sound forth towards it as a sign of understanding the macrocosmic World-Prayer of the fifth primeval Gospel which is connected with the Moon and Jupiter, even as the four Gospels are connected with the Earth . . . The 'Our Father' has been given to mankind as Prayer. There now resounds in answer to the microcosmic Paternoster, which was proclaimed from the east to the west, the primeval macrocosmic Prayer. So does it echoing sound, when, rightly understood by human souls, the prayer rings out into cosmic spaces and is given back with the words imprinted from out of the macrocosm. Let us take it with us, the macrocosmic Lord's Prayer, feeling that with it we begin to acquire understanding for the Gospel of Knowledge: the Fifth Gospel . . .

AUM, Amen!
The Evils hold sway,
Witness of Egoity becoming free,
Selfhood-Guilt through others incurred,
Experienced in the Daily Bread,
Wherein the Will of the Heavens does not rule,
In that Man severed himself from Your Kingdom,

And forgot Your Names,
Ye Fathers in the Heavens."

"AUM, Amen!
Es walten die Übel,
Zeugen sich lösender Ichheit,
Von andern erschuldete Selbstheitschuld,
Erlebet im täglichen Brote,
In dem nicht waltet der Himmel Wille,
Da der Mensch sich schied von Eurem Reich
Und vergass Euren Namen,
Ihr Väter in den Himmeln."

To emphasize the significance this macrocosmic Prayer had for Rudolf Steiner it is necessary to quote a sentence spoken by him one year later, on 19 September 1914,[10] in the Schreinerei:

"It was, my dear friends, one of the most sublime moments of my experience in the course of our Movement when for the first time I was allowed to utter the words:

Amen.
The Evils hold sway,
Witness of Egoity becoming free,
Selfhood-Guilt through others incurred,
Experienced in the Daily Bread,
Wherein the Will of the Heavens does not rule,
In that Man severed himself from Your Kingdom,
And forgot Your Names,
Ye Fathers in the Heavens."

By linking the Fifth Gospel with the laying of the Foundation Stone of the Goetheanum building, Rudolf Steiner accomplished a deed that stands like a Mystery in the history of our movement. He never mentioned this enigma again except two days after the laying of the Foundation Stone when on 22 September 1913 he said the following to the members in Basel: "The laying of the Foundation Stone must be experienced as a deed laden with responsibility for the very reason that we are justified in remembering it also as a laying of the corner stone for our consciousness that *that which we will* may take its place as a part of that which we feel to be the mission of the earth."[10]

These few words are immensely profound. They may be quoted as an example of the manner in which Rudolf Steiner entrusted spiritual correlations and background facts to the members. The one necessary condition is that each word and each sentence must be experienced in all its far-reaching significance.

In *The Fifth Gospel,*[11] at the beginning of October 1913, shortly after the laying of the Foundation Stone, Rudolf Steiner imparted facts from the Akashic Record about the life of Jesus, powerful spiritual proclamations which in later years he never took further or mentioned again. We must pay close attention to them in connection with the laying of the Foundation Stone and its place as part of the mission of the earth and must ask whether they shed any spiritual light on the events on the Dornach Hill.

In the Oslo lectures the life and being of Jesus of Nazareth are described. These lectures were preceded by the cycles on the Gospels, for instance *The Gospel of St. Luke*[12] and *The Gospel of St. Matthew.*[13] In both, the two Jesus children are mentioned. The Luke Gospel tells of a lofty spirit-soul who has never yet experienced an earthly life and who is born, therefore, as a young earth-soul, the *Adam Soul;* the other, described in the Matthew Gospel, is the reincarnated bearer of the highest earth wisdom and spiritual knowledge, Zarathustra. The two combine with one another. The ancient being of Zarathustra, imbued with depths of wisdom and knowledge, endowed with extraordinary spiritual purpose, leaves his body and as a leading individuality, rich in earth experience, enters the young soul of the twelve year-old boy in the Gospel of Luke. As described in *The Fifth Gospel,* Jesus travelled as a carpenter throughout Palestine. His most unusual schooling was to learn about contemporary human life expressed in the spiritual streams, the political and legal disputes and social troubles of that time. He gained deep insights into the burdens of existence. His greatest anguish was occasioned by the dissolution of the spiritual cults. From their ancient origins of highest Mystery guidance they had degenerated into acts of hideous demonic possession and become the source of spiritual and human decline and downfall.

In such glimpses into the demonised cult atmosphere, Jesus experienced a view of most terrible abysses, the feeling of absolute helplessness and impotence coupled with infinite pity for the hopelessness of the situation in which mankind found itself.

While experiencing one such cult he was overwhelmed by the horror of what was going on; in a kind of initiation shock he heard the voice of wisdom which was the voice of the transformed *Bath Kol* proclaiming from out of the sun region the truth about the link that no longer existed between man and the divine beings who were his guides. The words he heard were those of the ancient macrocosmic Prayer, known in all the ancient Mysteries, words which were spoken by Rudolf Steiner for the first time during the laying of the Foundation Stone (See p. 20).

Thus was Jesus initiated into the knowledge of the evils, the knowledge of the path taken by the ego when it severed its links with the spiritual world and forgot the fathers in heaven.

Both the Jesus-Zarathustra individuality and the Adam Soul of Jesus suffered infinite pain during this experience of initiation showing the culminating horror of the spiritual ruin of mankind. This led to the spiritual maturity and inner consecration that made possible the heights of ultimate sacrifice. Round about the thirtieth year the Zarathustra Ego departed from the body he had inhabited since his twelfth year on earth. In the river Jordan, John baptised the body of Jesus from which the Zarathustra Ego had departed.

At the moment of baptism, Christ the Sun Spirit, the World Ego, entered into the Jesus sheath which contained the Adam Soul. For three years this spirit permeated this earthly human body with divinity. Out of occult necessity, at the behest of the spiritual world, Rudolf Steiner gave to the Anthroposophical Society in the lectures of the Fifth Gospel, the Gospel of Knowledge, something which radiates out into the world. In the course of many years of contemplation this can build bridges to an understanding of deeply hidden interrelationships which culminated in the Christmas Conference.

In order to bring these spiritual interrelations into a closer connection let us turn our attention once again to the laying of the Foundation Stone in 1913. As mentioned above, the speaking of the inverted Lord's Prayer must be seen as an absolutely essential deed within the framework of this act. So the Foundation Stone of the Goetheanum is linked with the initiation knowledge received by the Zarathustra-Adam-Jesus Being. The inner path trodden by Jesus from the moment of the initiation shock he experienced at the altar of the heathen at the age of twenty-four, right up to the Baptism in the Jordan, is described in the Fifth Gospel and plays a part in forming the spiritual aura for the laying of the Foundation Stone. The laying of the Foundation Stone commences with the speaking of the Prayer of knowledge of the evils that hold sway, witnessing the freeing of egoity. This is a revelation of the grounds of truth known to the Mysteries since time immemorial. This mystery truth is spoken aloud beside the hollow awaiting the Foundation Stone. Because the time is ripe and the souls of men are ready, something that has hitherto been deeply veiled is now entrusted to the consciousness soul. The consciousness soul receives the baptism of knowledge at the Mystery site of the 20th century, the Dornach Hill. A little over ten years from that moment, the Christ statue was to have been placed in the far end of the small dome. This figure in wood, nine metres high, depicts Christ striding among mankind, striding westward, while the evils that hold sway among men, Lucifer and Ahriman, seem to be smashed as they touch Him. That was to have been the task of the Goetheanum itself, its permanent and abiding goal.

Having touched on the great images of the laying of the Foundation Stone, when the crystalline body of copper with its twice times twelve five-sided surfaces was laid into the limestone of the Jura hills, let us now consider the experience of a visitor to the Goetheanum. Entering from the west, he stands in the great hall looking eastwards. There he would have seen, striding towards him, Christ with His gesture of love. The evil from above is shattered by the upward reaching arm while the evil from below, from the depths, entangles itself and is shackled by the earthward pointing arm.

On 6 October 1913 in the fifth lecture of *The Fifth Gospel,* Rudolf Steiner uttered something that was living in the soul of Christ-Jesus: "And then there dawned in Him as the earthly experience of the God: What I have to tell human beings is not how the gods prepared the path from the spirit to the earth, but how men can find the path leading upwards from the earth to the spirit."[11] This is the word of the spirit rising from the Foundation Stone to the Christ statue, a word that has become the *leitmotiv* of the Michaelic spirit of the age.

Before Rudolf Steiner gave his address, he read aloud the Foundation Stone document which was then soldered into the copper Foundation Stone. In an article entitled *Recollections in Commemoration of the Laying of the Foundation Stone of the First Goetheanum on 20 September 1913,* Nelly Grosheintz-Lavall gave an impressive and lively account of what happened at that time.

"I should like to describe in simple terms the ceremony of the laying of the Foundation Stone on the physical plane. Indeed I must start further back in time and explain briefly why this Building, which had been planned for Munich, came to be erected on what was then an untouched hillside that had been known for centuries as Blood Hill (harking back to the Battle of Dornach in 1499).

"Here we owned two hectares of land on which stood our summer house Brodbeck, since converted and enlarged and now known as Rudolf Steiner Halde. After the Basel lecture cycle on the Gospel of St. Mark in the autumn of 1912, Fräulein von Sivers together with her sister Olga and Fräulein Waller spent a few days rest there while Dr. Steiner paid visits to Edouard Schure in Baar (Alsace) and Christian Morgenstern in Graubünden. After this they intended to proceed to Italy.

"Frau Dr. Steiner — then Fraulein von Sivers — reported as

follows about this first stay there in the Nachrichtenblatt of 16 August 1925:

" 'The hill was green and virgin, uneven and untouched except for the north-western slope where stood Haus Brodbeck . . . In brilliant autumn sunshine the landscape spread out before us; the cherry trees flamed red in the valley, like fire, blood burning in the play of the sunshine . . . Round about the Dornach Hill the slopes shone in every shade of yellow. For us city dwellers it was a delightful view. Thrilled, I leaned out of the window. But next morning Rudolf Steiner awoke as he had never been before. For apparently no reason he was bewildered, crushed, gloomy. Something like this never happened to him, for despite the endless bustle and hurry he was harmonious and even-tempered. It passed; yet I had the feeling, which has recurred many times since then, that in that first night he foresaw many things which he had to forbid himself to turn over in his thoughts.'

"To everybody's astonishment, Dr. Steiner stayed in Dornach, exploring the whole district and even climbing into the Arlesheim caves.

"Then he called on us in Basel and the following conversation took place:

"Dr. Steiner: 'What do you plan to do with this piece of land?'

"Dr. Grosheintz: 'When I bought it, I said to my wife that the future will reveal why I had to buy so much land.'

"Myself: 'I should like us to build a boarding school where children can grow up in the right way.'

"Thereupon Dr. Steiner spoke the fateful words: 'We have been thinking about a kind of Bayreuth.'

"We knew about the troubles being encountered in Munich, so my husband answered: 'Dornach has no building restrictions —"

"And Dr. Steiner added: 'And Basel has a favourable theosophical karma.'

"And then he told us about the steps taken in Munich, which were turning out to be nothing but a waste of time. He said what he so often repeated later on: 'We have no time to waste.'

"At the end of February 1913 planning permission was again

refused by the building authorities in Munich. Shortly after this the Johannes-Bau Verein decided to erect the building on our hill. Since we only owned the front portion of the land — where the Building now stands — we realized that we would have to purchase the rear portion in addition.

"Our friends from Zurich and Bern, Professor Gisi, Frau Hirter-Weber and Frau Schieb, made it possible for the present parcel of land to become a Swiss Foundation.

"I feel it is important to mention that all this took place at the suggestion of Dr. Steiner. For us to have taken the initiative for this change of plan would have seemed like a betrayal of our dear devoted Munich members. We sensed how grievously they must feel the loss of the Building for which the land had already been acquired.

"I was grateful to Frau Dr. Wegman when she said to me: 'If anyone should say to you that it is wrong to build here, then tell them this: In 1905 I (Dr. Wegman) was on may way from Holland to Zurich where I intended to start studying medicine. I broke my journey in Berlin, where I was able to hear Dr. Steiner speak and I asked Fräulein von Sivers whether I had not better study in Berlin, where I should be able to attend all Dr. Steiner's lectures. But she said that I should go to Zurich, adding that our whole movement would eventually find itself in Switzerland.' Prophetic words in 1905!

"Thanks to this advice from Fräulein von Sivers, Dr. Wegman turned out to be the only doctor among the members who had Swiss qualifications which enabled her, in Switzerland after the war, to assist Dr. Steiner in the practical renewal of medicine.

"Fateful words, too, for the whole work of Anthroposophy! They show how hidden within karma lay the very remedy which was to protect the Building intended as a homeland for souls. Fräulein von Sivers' words also point to the degree of danger that for a time threatened the Movement of Rudolf Steiner.

"In 1911 the lodges of German theosophists in Switzerland were informed that the four Geneva lodges, attached to Paris, had reorganized themselves into seven lodges in order to gain a national charter, which had been promptly granted by Mrs. Besant. Thus there was now a national committee in Geneva which was responsible for the administration of all the theosophical lodges in Switzerland. This committee was to consist of the seven chairmen of the seven founding lodges. In accordance with the statutes of the Theosophical Society at that time, the general secretary of a section could not speak without invitation in the area covered by another section. The aim of reorganizing the Geneva lodges was thus to prevent Dr. Steiner from lecturing in Switzerland. Dr. Emil Grosheintz had to fight a tough battle before Mrs. Besant agreed to withdraw the Swiss charter and permit the Swiss German lodges to be recognized as belonging to Dr. Rudolf Steiner's stream.

"It is necessary to remind ourselves of these matters. The souls of those who bore responsibility for the work were expanded and strengthened by their awareness of these obstacles, oppositions and battles.

"Their mood was grave as the moment of the laying of the Foundation Stone approached. I would have said grave and full of cares, except that the being of Rudolf Steiner himself raised us above those cares. We knew we would gain the strength to cope with them.

"The memorable day dawned. Dr. Steiner had announced it only three days beforehand, so not many people heard about it. On the day of the announcement, in the evening, Dr. Steiner dug out the first few spadefuls of earth and the members present then proceeded to dig. For the next two days this digging was continued feverishly, during the daytime by the workmen and in the evening by the members.

"On 20 September the pit was ready. Nine steps led down into the depths where a cemented smaller hollow would receive the Foundation Stone.

"The ceremony was planned for 6:30 in the evening, but could not start till 7 o'clock. The day passed in expectant mood. The Foundation Stone had been brought. It consisted of two copper dodecahedra, one larger than the other, soldered together and not quite one meter long. Rudolf Steiner himself had given the measurements.

Later, Engineer Englert told me that after the laying of the Foundation Stone Rudolf Steiner calculated the measurements of the building. The calculation did not quite work out; there was a remainder. But then he noticed that the measurements of the Foundation Stone accounted for this remainder.

"The parchment for the document, made from the skin of a male calf, had been provided by Graf Lerchenfeld. During the afternoon, Dr. Steiner was busy writing the inscription. Later he read this aloud to us.

"The sky had clouded over during the day and when we were all gathered a great wind arose. Thunder rumbled in the distance, lightning again and again rent the darkness and the landscape seemed eerie.

"A fine drizzle started to fall while Dr. Steiner was reading the document aloud. But the full thunder storm with pouring rain only broke after the conclusion of the ceremony. For the participants the subsequent release of the elements became inextricably merged with the immense and shattering impressions of the ceremony itself; this was apparent later in many a later description of the event.

"The Foundation Stone was carried on outstretched arms by Dr. Peipers while two members steadied it by holding long straps. It was borne down the nine steps to its resting place. It was laid with the larger dodecahedron pointing eastwards and the smaller westwards — the opposite of the Building.

"Fräulein von Sivers laid a bouquet of roses, twelve red and one white, on the Foundation Stone which was then covered with earth by Architect Schmidt and Engineer Englert.

"Then Dr. Steiner joined hands cross-wise with those surrounding the Foundation Stone — Fräulein von Sivers, Fräulein Stinde, Dr. Grosheintz, Dr. Peipers, Architect Schmidt and Engineer Englert, after which they all left the pit, Dr. Steiner last.

"Then Dr. Steiner gave the address. He spoke of the answer that can be given to an audible cry for the spirit wherever spiritual science can work with its gospel, the knowledge of the spirit. It would be possible to proclaim the Fifth Gospel if human souls could find their way towards understanding. As the first item from this Fifth Gospel, Dr. Steiner read aloud the macrocosmic Prayer, 'The evils hold sway' as a counter-image of the microcosmic Lord's Prayer."[14]

Fritz Edelmann[15] made a shorthand record of the address given by Rudolf Steiner at the laying of the Foundation Stone of the Johannes Building in Dornach on 20 September 1913. Like a universal seed these words were laid into the spiritual sheath of the Dornach Hill.

"We begin our task. — (Turning towards east, south, west, north and at each turn calling a name):

"You Seraphim, you Cherubim, you Rulers of the World, and you high Thrones who like lightning through the spiritual streams take up the sheaths of the Cherubim, wedding them to make the creative existence of the world: we call on you to guard our deed. You Wisdoms . . . , you guardians of the eternal universal forces, and you Formers of our Existence who pour the form of all being into the streams of existence: we call on you to guard our deed. And you Personalities of the spiritual stream, and you Helpers, Archangeloi and Angeloi, who are for the earth the messengers of the spiritual life of man: We call on all of you to guard and guide this our deed. We call you down upon man's soul which we will consecrate in so far as we are called upon to do so. We draw near to this soul of man which we will dedicate to that Work which, according to our best knowledge of the times, will give its services.

"As an image of the human soul which dedicates itself to our great Work we have shaped this Stone. In its double twelvefoldness it is for us an image of the striving human soul, a microcosm planted in the macrocosm. Anthropos, Man as descendent of Beings of the divine spiritual hierarchies. So this our Corner Stone is image of our own soul which we incorporate into that which we have recognized as the right spiritual striving for the present time. So we shall plant this Stone, formed according to the univeral images of the human soul, into the kingdom of the elements. Within this Stone there are two minerals, taken from the condensed kingdom of the elements, which best express how the forces of the macrocosm work together in the condensed realm of the elements. This twelvefoldness, as the proper sign of the human soul, we shall plant this very evening in the spot above which shall rise that which shall become a sign to us of our work, my dear theosophical friends. And with this Stone we shall plant that through which we dedicate ourselves to what we have recognized to be right in our spiritual life.

"This Document will be planted within our Stone. It bears the inscription '*In the name* of the Seraphim, the Cherubim, the Thrones, the Wisdoms, the Movers, the Formers, the Personalities, the Archai, the Archangeloi, the Angeloi!'

"In the Macrocosm as a microcosm lives man, *Anthropos,* depicted here too as a twice twelvefold image, symbol of the spiritual world. And within this symbol the words of Rosicrucianism, well known to you my dear friends, give expression to the meaning of our striving: (E.D.N. I.C.M. P.S.S.R.) Ex deo nascimur. In Christo morimur. Per spiritum sanctum reviviscimus.

"We must understand correctly: As a formula of dedication it is written here on this Stone which as a *Corner Stone* expresses the human being who wills to seek himself in the spirit, who senses himself in the World-I. This Stone we lower into the kingdom of the condensed elements as symbol of the force for which we endeavour to strive through 3, 5, 7, 12, laid by the Johannes-Bau Verein, Dornach, on the 20th day of September 1880 after the Mystery of Golgotha, that is 1913 after the Birth of Christ, when Mercury as the evening star stood in Libra.

As Architect:
Carl Schmid-Curtius

As Administrative Council
of the Johannes-Bau Verein:

Stinde	Frau Burgi
Grosheintz	Frau Schieb
Linde	Frau Hirter-Weber
Peipers	

Kalckreuth
Unger
Gumppenberg

As Central Vorstand of the
Anthroposophical Society:
von Sivers
Unger
and Dr. Steiner
as spiritual leader of the ceremony.

"This document is incorporated within the symbol of the human soul and then in the condensed kingdom of the elements. — (The document is placed in the container of sheet copper which is then closed by soldering.)

"The Stone, symbol of our soul, is laid into the condensed kingdom of the elements. — (The Stone is carried by Dr. Peipers and held by long straps by two men. It is taken to the spot where it is to rest. It is laid with the larger dodecahedron to the east, the smaller to the west, that is the opposite of the Building whose larger dome points westward and the smaller eastward.)

"The Stone as symbol of our soul has been laid in the earth; may it be a token of striving for knowledge, for love, for strong action, a symbol of mankind. For our soul it shall be a token that resounds henceforth from the deepest meaning of the world word: Ex deo nascimur. In Christo morimur. Per spiritum sanctum reviviscimus.

"The symbol of the human soul shall become a token of the human soul. With the first strokes made upon this our True Building I consecrate you to be a token of the human soul. — (3, 5, 7 strokes upon the small body, 12 strokes upon the large body.) — The Stone has now been transformed from symbol to token. And now let us entrust it to the kingdom of the condensed elements, the earth, into which our soul was lowered so that it might develop through human evolution that which was to be its earth mission. The Stone is no longer a token;

The first Goetheanum

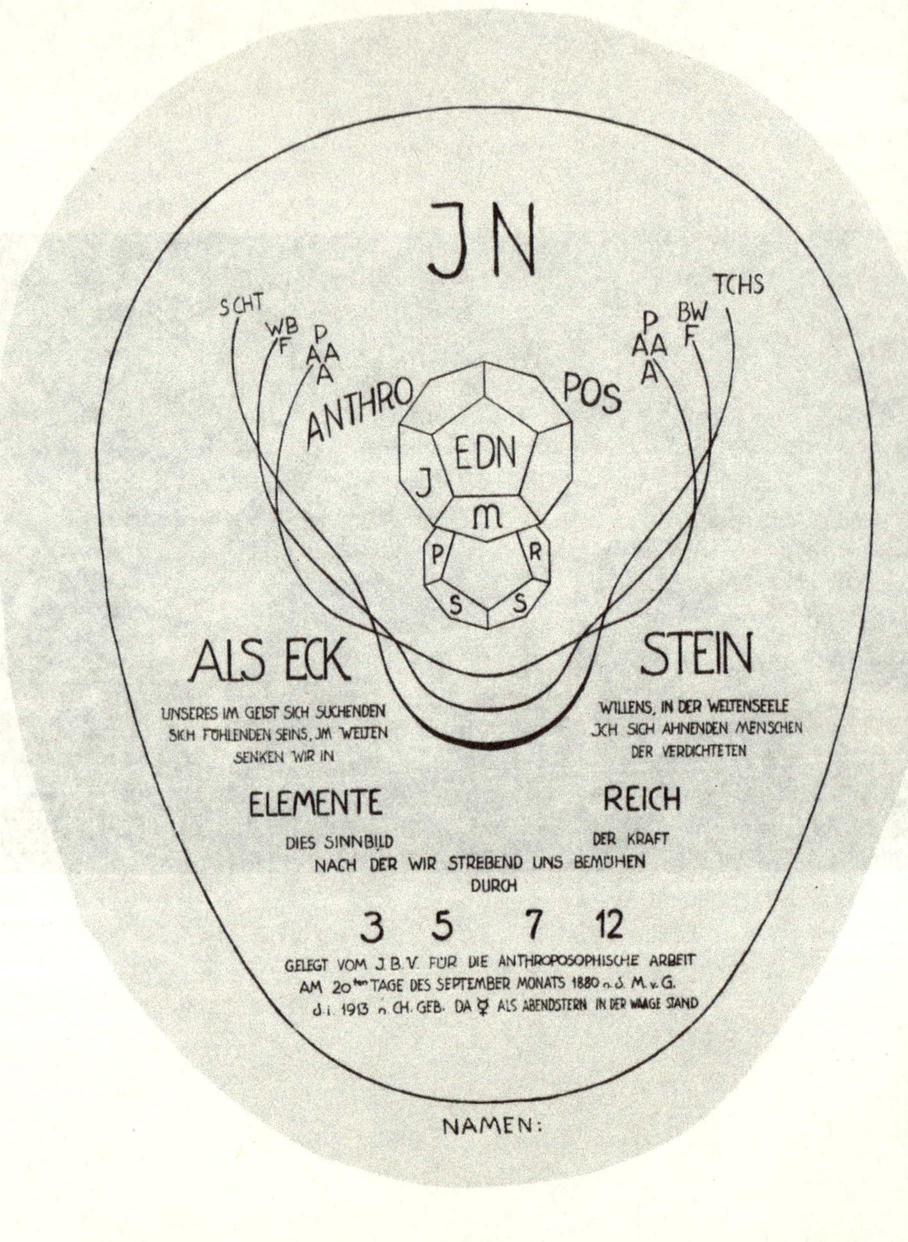

The Foundation Stone document drawn by Rudolf Stiner. Length 130 cm, width 90 cm.

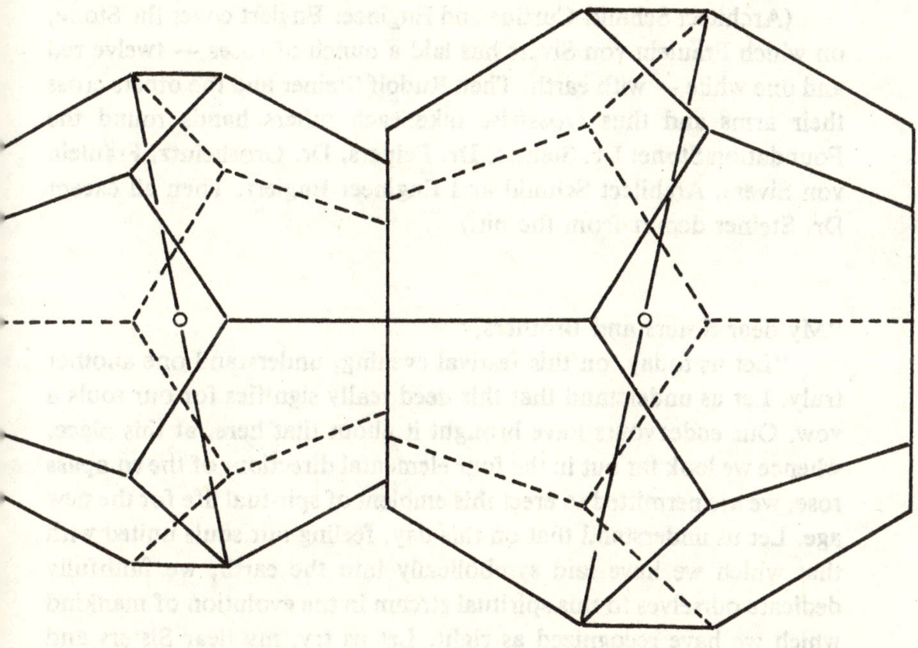

The two dodecahedra of the Foundation Stone made of copper. Combined length 96 cm. A Pyrite crystal is suspended in the centre of each; in the larger body the smaller crystal and in the smaller body the larger crystal.

it is sheathed when we entrust it to the earth. Thrice the human soul rises up to the three secrets of existence: First they are symbols; then they are tokens when the soul reads the eternal world word; but the profoundest depths of the world secrets are vividly bound to the soul when this soul is able to create its own sheath out of the kingdom of the hierarchies. — So be sheathed! First symbol, then token, now sheathed so that you may become a firm Corner Stone of our striving, for our seeking inasmuch as we have seen it to be right in the evolution of mankind. Let us make of the Stone that is a token of our soul one that is sheathed."

(Architect Schmid-Curtius and Engineer Englert cover the Stone, on which Fräulein von Sivers has laid a bunch of roses — twelve red and one white — with earth. Then Rudolf Steiner and the others cross their arms and thus crosswise take each others hands round the Foundation Stone: Dr. Steiner, Dr. Peipers, Dr. Grosheintz, Fräulein von Sivers, Architect Schmid and Engineer Englert. Then all except Dr. Steiner depart from the pit.)

"My dear Sisters and Brothers,

"Let us today, on this festival evening, understand one another truly. Let us understand that this deed really signifies for our souls a vow. Our endeavours have brought it about that here, at this place, whence we look far out in the four elemental directions of the compass rose, we are permitted to erect this emblem of spiritual life for the new age. Let us understand that on this day, feeling our souls united with that which we have laid symbolically into the earth, we faithfully dedicate ourselves to this spiritual stream in the evolution of mankind which we have recognized as right. Let us try, my dear Sisters and Brothers, to make this vow in our souls: that in this moment we will look away from all the minutiae of life, from all that binds us — must of necessity bind us — as human beings to the daily round. Let us try in this moment to awaken in ourselves the thought of all that links the human soul with the striving of the Turning Point Of Time. Let us try to think for a moment that , as we do what we have vowed to do this evening, we must bear within us the consciousness of looking into far, far cycles of time, in order to become aware of how the mission, of which this Building is to be the emblem, will take its place in the great mission of mankind upon our planet earth. Not in pride and vainglory — in humility, devotion and readiness for sacrifice, let us try to lift our souls to the great plans, the great purposes of man's activity on earth. Let us try to put ourselves into the position in which we really ought to be and must be if we understand this moment aright.

"Let us try to think how there once entered into our earth-evolution the great announcement, the great communication, the primeval, eternal Gospel of divine-spiritual life, how it passed over the earth at a time when the divine spirits themselves were still the great teachers of mankind. Let us try, my dear Sisters and Brothers, to transfer ourselves back into those sacred ages of earth-existence, of which a last yearning, a very last memory still dawns on us when, maybe in ancient Greece, with the last echoes of the mystery-wisdom and simultaneously with the first tones of philosophy, we listen to their great Plato telling of the eternal forms and the eternal substance of the world. And let us try to grasp what since those times has spread over our earth-evolution as luciferic and ahrimanic influences. Let us try to make clear to ourselves how the connection with the divine cosmic existence, with the willing, with the feeling and with the divine-spiritual knowing, has faded from the human soul.

"Let us try in this moment to feel deep, deep in our own souls what in the countries of the east, the north, the west, the south, those human souls whom we acknowledge as the noblest are feeling today, though they get no further than, let us say, a vague, inadequate longing and hoping for the spirit. Look around you, my dear Sisters and Brothers, and see how this undefined longing, this vague hoping for the spirit prevails throughout mankind today. Feel, and harken, here by the Foundation Stone of our emblem, how in the vague yearning and hoping of mankind for the spirit, there is audible the cry for the answer, for that answer which can be given where Spiritual Science can be present, with its Gospel of the Knowledge of the Spirit. Try to engrave into your souls the greatness of the moment through which we are passing this evening. If we can hear the longing call of mankind for the spirit and resolve to erect the true Building from out of which the tidings of the spirit shall ever more and more be proclaimed — if we feel this in the life of this our world, then we understand one another truly this evening. Then we know — not in pride and nowise over-valuing our own efforts, but in humility, in devotion and readiness for sacrifice — that in our indefatigable endeavours we must be the continuers of that spiritual work which has been extinguished in the west in the course of advancing human evolution. Inevitably, through the adverse influence of the ahrimanic forces, that evolution ended by bringing mankind to the point where we stand today, the point where souls could only wither and waste away, should that cry of longing for the spirit go unheard. My dear Sisters and Brothers, let us feel this anxiety! It must be so if — aglow with the fire of love — we are to fight on in that great spiritual conflict it was granted us to inherit, in that great spiritual conflict which was when they repelled the Ahrimanic onslaught of the Moors.

"Led by karma, we stand at this moment at a place through which important streams of spiritual life have flowed; let us feel within ourselves this evening the full gravity of the situation. Mankind in days gone by had reached the culminating point in its striving for personality. When in the fullness of this earthly personality, the ancient heritage, received from the divine leaders of the very beginning of earth-evolution, had exhausted itself, then in the east the Cosmic Word appeared:

In the Beginning was the Word
And the Word was with God
And a God was the Word.

"And the Word was made manifest to the souls of men and spoke to the souls of men: Fill earth-evolution with the purpose and meaning of the earth! Now the Word Itself has passed over into the earth-aura, has been received into the spiritual aura of the earth.

"Fourfold has been the proclamation of the Cosmic Word through the centuries numbering now well-nigh two thousand years. Thus has the light of cosmic worlds shone into earth-evolution.

"Deeper and ever deeper Ahriman sank, and had perforce to sink. Let us feel ourselves surrounded by the souls of men in whom the cry of yearning for the spirit resounds. But let us feel, my dear Sisters and Brothers, how these human souls all round us might be left crying out in vain, since Ahriman, dark Ahriman, is spreading chaos over all spiritual knowledge of the worlds of the higher hierarchies for which they strive. Feel that in our time the possibility has indeed arisen of adding to the spirit-word, four times proclaimed, that other proclamation which I can now present, but in a symbol only.

"From the east it came — the light and the Word of the proclamation. From out of the east it passed over to the west, four times proclaimed in the four Gospels; awaiting the advent from the west of the mirror that will add knowledge to what is still only proclamation in the four times uttered Cosmic Word. It pierces deeply into our hearts and souls when we listen to that Sermon on the Mount, which was uttered in the hour when the time for the ripening of human personality was fulfilled, when the ancient light of the spirit had vanished and the new spirit-light appeared. The new spirit-light has appeared! But after it appeared, it travelled through the centuries of human evolution from east to west, waiting for understanding of the words which once in the Sermon on the Mount had sounded their way into human hearts. Deep-toned rings out of the depths of our cosmic evolution that immemorial, undying Prayer, uttered as proclamation of the cosmic word when the Mystery of Golgotha was enacted. Deep-toned rang out the undying Prayer which from the innermost core of the human heart was to make known to the microcosm, in depths of soul, the secret of existence. That secret was to be heard in the Lord's Prayer, as we know it, and as it reverberated from east towards west. Yet it waited patiently, this cosmic word which sank then into the microcosm — waited in order that one day it might resound in harmony with the Fifth Gospel; for the souls of men had to mature before they could understand that which as the most ancient of all, because it is the Macrocosmic Gospel, is now to reverberate from the west like an echo to the Gospel of the east.

"If we bring understanding to this present moment, then understanding will also dawn in us that to the Four Gospels a Fifth Gospel can be added. So, on this present evening, may there ring forth in addition to the secrets of the Microcosm, the words which express the secrets of the Macrocosm. As a first revelation of the Fifth Gospel there shall even now sound forth the macrocosmic counter-image of the microcosmic Prayer that was once proclaimed from east to west. So let sound forth towards it as a sign of understanding the macrocosmic World-Prayer of the Fifth primeval Gospel which is connected with the Moon and Jupiter, even as the four Gospels are connected with the earth:

AUM, Amen!
The Evils hold sway,
Witness of Egoity becoming free,
Selfhood-Guilt through others incurred,
Experienced in the Daily Bread,
Wherein the Will of the Heavens does not rule.
In that Man severed himself from Your Kingdom,
And forgot Your Names,
Ye Fathers in the Heavens.

"The 'Our Father' had been given to mankind as Prayer. There now resounds in answer to the microcosmic Paternoster, which was proclaimed from the east to the west, the primeval macrocosmic Prayer. So does it echoing sound, when, rightly understood by human souls, the Prayer rings out into cosmic spaces and is given back with the words imprinted from out of the macrocosm. Let us take it with us, the macrocosmic Lord's Prayer, feeling that with it we begin to acquire understanding for the Gospel of Knowledge: the Fifth Gospel. From this grave moment let us take home earnestly and worthily in our souls: our Will. Let us take home the certainty that all wisdom for which the human soul is seeking — if the seeking be true — is a reflex of cosmic wisdom; and that it makes fruitful from out of the love that is sovereign in the evolution of mankind all of human love that is rooted in the soul's own selfless love.

"Throughout all earthly ages and into all men's souls there works, out of strong human will that has filled itself with the meaning of existence and the meaning of the earth, a further strengthening — a strengthening through the cosmic power for which men crave today, casting uncertain glances towards a spirit for which they hope — but which they refuse to know, because Ahriman has buried an unconscious fear in the human soul, wherever the spirit is spoken of today. Let us feel this, my Sisters and Brothers, at this moment. Feel this, and you will be able to arm yourselves for your spiritual task and as revealers of the spirit-light 'will prove yourselves strong in thought, even in the hour when dark Ahriman, clouding wisdom, means to spread the darkness of chaos over fully-awakened spiritual sight'.

"My Sisters and Brothers, fill your souls with the longing for real knowledge of the spirit, for true human love, for strength of will. And try to quicken in yourselves that spirit which has trust in the utterance of the Cosmic Word as it echoes to us out of cosmic distances and out of the wide expanse of space, sounding into our souls. This is what one who has grasped the meaning of existence must truly feel in this evening hour: Human souls have reached the limit of their striving. Feel in humility, not in pride, in devotion and willingness for sacrifice, not in arrogant presumption, what is to come of the emblem for which we have laid the Foundation Stone today. Feel this portent of the knowledge which should come to us because it is given to us to know: In our time, the veil enshrouding the spiritual beings in the expanses of space must be pierced through, as the spiritual beings come to speak to us of the meaning of existence. Everywhere, everywhere in the surrounding world the souls of men must needs receive into themselves the meaning of existence. Hear how, in whatever cultural centres there is talk of or knowledge of the spirit, of religion, of art, the energies of souls are growing more and more barren. Feel how you must learn to quicken these souls, these energies, out of Imaginations, Inspirations, Intuitions of the spirit. Feel what he will find who hears aright the ring of creative spirituality.

"Those who in addition to the old Lord's Prayer learn to understand the meaning of the Prayer from the Fifth Gospel, they will recognize the root of that meaning out of the Turning Point of our Time.

"If we learn to understand the meaning of these words, we shall seek to receive into ourselves the seeds that must blossom now if earth-evolution is not to wither, if it is still to bear fruit and thrive, so that through the will of man the earth can reach the goal set her from the very beginning.

"Feel, then, this evening, that the wisdom and the meaning of the new knowledge, of the new love and of the great new strength must come alive in the souls of men. The souls who will be working amid the blossoming and the fruits of future ages of earth-evolution will have to understand that which we today mean to implant in our souls for the first time: the macrocosmic voice of the ageless, eternal Prayer, sounding towards us.

AUM, Amen!
The Evils hold sway,
Witness of Egoity becoming free,
Selfhood-Guilt through others incurred,
Experienced in the Daily Bread,
Wherein the Will of the Heavens does not rule,
In that Man severed himself from Your Kingdom,
Ye Fathers in the Heavens.

"Thus we will go our separate ways — taking with us in our souls the consciousness of the meaning of the earnestness and the dignity

of the solemn act we have performed. The consciousness which remains of this evening shall kindle in us the striving for knowledge of a new revelation given to mankind, for which the human soul thirsts, from which it will drink. But only then when, without fear, it wins faith and confidence in what the Science of the Spirit can make known, the Science that is to unite once more those three that, for a time, perforce took their several roads through the evolution of mankind: Religion, Art and Science. Let us take this with us, my Sisters and Brothers, as a memory of this hour we have celebrated together, and as something we would wish never to forget."[9]
(Then the Foundation Stone was covered over and cemented in.)

Let us now examine in detail the document that had been placed inside the pentagon-dodecahedron. Rudolf Steiner had made a drawing showing a double pentagon-dodecahedron in a vertical position. This is surrounded by an egg-shaped line which encloses the whole drawing like a sheath. Above the pentagon-dodecahedron are two large letters: J N. In his address Rudolf Steiner gave the full meaning of the various abbreviations and named the hierarchies in the sequence in which they appear, indicated by letters that are linked by curved lines that surround the pentagon-dodecahedron like a chalice:

"In the Name (J N) of the Seraphim, the Cherubim, the Thrones (S CH T), the Wisdoms, the Movers (Beweger), the Formers (W B F), the Personalities, the Archai, the Archangeloi, the Angeloi (P AA A)

AS A CORNER STONE
of our Will that seeks itself in the Spirit,
of our Being that feels itself in the World Soul,
of the Human Being who senses himself in the World I,
we lower into the condensed
elements' kingdom
this Symbol of the force

for which we endeavour to strive
through
3 5 7 12

laid by the J B V for the work of Anthroposophy on the 20th day of September 1880 after the Mystery of Golgotha, that is 1913 after the Birth of Christ when Mercury as the evening star stood in Libra."

Names: . . ."

(J B V = Johannes-Bau Verein; n. d. M. v. G. = nach dem Mysterium von Golgatha = after the Mystery of Golgotha; n. Chr. Geb = nach Christi Geburt = after Christ's birth; 3 5 7 12 = strokes with the hammer).

All other abbreviations and the names of those signing the document were read out by Rudolf Steiner during the course of the ceremony. Whenever we contemplate the drawing we find that questions arise and also the strong feeling that it has more to say than can be expressed in just reading it aloud. This is specially the case with the two letters which so conspicuously dominate the cosmic form language of the drawing: J N. Rudolf Steiner read out "In the Name of . . ." but they remind us strongly also of "Jesus Nazarenus". And the whole ceremony does indeed cause our thoughts to turn to this personality, since in a most profound and mysterious way the revelation of the Fifth Gospel is linked with the laying of the Foundation Stone of the Goetheanum. Most strongly of all the cosmic "Our Father" is linked with it.

One year after the laying of the Foundation Stone, on 19 September 1914, Rudolf Steiner said in an address which recalled the event:

"On that occasion I was able to utter for the first time those words, which I do not simply imagine I know, but am absolutely convinced that they were in very truth heard out of the divine heights, uttered by that being who was to be the bearer of the Christ Who would lead mankind to harmony. It was, my dear friends, one of the most sublime moments of my experience in the course of our Movement, when for the first time I was allowed to utter the words:

Amen — AUM
The Evils hold sway,
Witness of Egoity becoming free,
Selfhood-Guilt through others incurred,
Experienced in the Daily Bread,
Wherein the Will of the Heavens does not rule,
In that Man severed himself from Your Kingdom,
And forgot Your Names,
Ye Fathers in the Heavens.

"In these words — as will be gradually apparent to him who considers them often enough — is contained something lofty and ennobling, moving human hearts and souls. In them, however, is also something which can saturate human hearts and souls with pain and sorrow. In them, too, if allowed to work rightly in the soul, is contained a force which can uphold our spiritual Stream and endow it with an inner certainty in whatever position of life we may find ourselves, and whatever conditions of life we are required to meet."[10]

Straight after the laying of the Foundation Stone the third general meeting of the Johannes-Bau Verein took place in Basel on 22 September 1913. Rudolf Steiner spoke urgently about the ceremony of 20 September: "The Stone we bore in our hands during the ceremony is linked in the first place with the symbol of our soul which we entrust, in a way, to the mission of the earth. Furthermore, we are right in stressing on this occasion that this Stone is intended to be the Corner Stone of something which must be for us an answer to a general cry that is present at the moment in the spiritual life of mankind . . .

"Then we shall sense that we have made of this Stone a token of what our present time so urgently needs: an answer to the cry of the human soul struggling with the fear of knowledge. Only then will we feel the earnestness that is required. We know what we have to do and why *this stone, which is intended to denote knowledge, love and great strength* will have to become for many of those who are against us a stumbling block and a bone of contention. Let us not imagine that our difficult days are over. I certainly do not want to give that impression; but may our souls grow strong in the trust that we shall overcome the difficulties. Toad natures will appear from under every stone and for them this Building will be a stumbling block and a bone of contention. Therefore we shall have to be properly watchful and courageous in holding our position! Perhaps this laying of the Stone will be only the beginning of what we have to achieve for truth and by way of standing up for the truth. For this reason I am anxious to explain to you in words what I was able to tell you about for the first time, my dear friends, during the laying of the Foundation Stone. I want to explain to you in words what might be called the macrocosmic echo of that Prayer *which may be approached as the most important event of this fourth period of our post-Atlantean development.* Then out of the mysterious script of the Fifth Gospel will gradually be revealed what will have to be added to the other Gospels during the fifth period. Then the eternal Prayer which is a part of the Gospels and which sounds in the microcosm as the 'Our Father' will come towards us out of the Fifth Gospel as the 'Our Father' of knowledge — instead of the 'Our Father' of man's supplication for redemption. That which is a supplication for redemption in the fourth period is knowledge in the fifth period."[10]

To say that the *Fifth Gospel* surrounds the laying of the Foundation Stone like an aura is to point to those mysterious links that exist between the Turning Point Of Time and the ceremony on the Dornach Hill. This is said clearly by Rudolf Steiner in the words already quoted (p. 21): "that that which we will may take its place as part of that which we feel to be the mission of the earth." So it is all-important to gain a clear picture of "that which we will" so that it may be given its place in the mission of the earth.

It is the mission of the earth to become the Planet of Love, just as once it was the mission of Old Moon to become the Planet of Wisdom. Though the mission of the earth can be formulated thus concisely, there is obviously a tremendous amount to be done even to gain a view of what *Planet of Love* might mean, let alone form a more or less clear conception of it.

To become a Planet of Love is a univeral, cosmic goal. And those who stand in the midst of this cosmic task are the human beings who devote their many, many past and future earth lives to this goal. As they are today they have as yet realized only a tiny fraction of the power of love within themselves. Most human actions today reveal man's weakness and inability to be a bearer or giver of love. Man's greatest affliction is the fact that he is unable to give what he himself most longs and yearns for: love. Too much coldness and anti-love live in him, expressed in egoism, burdening and withering the life that flows between people. Man alone would never be capable of winning the greatest of all forces if that Being had not come to him whose nature, whose very substance, is love to be poured into mankind. Man cannot be truly man if he does not partake of this divine substance of love. The Bringer of Love had to bring Himself and sacrifice Himself totally in mankind. There can only be sacrifice where there is love. We speak of the Sun Being of Christ and His sacrifice, the Mystery of Golgotha. Since the Turning Point Of Time earthly man has lived within the sacrificial force of Christ's love. It surrounds man like the air he breathes; it rouses him to be a man when he absorbs the Christ impulse, it absorbs him and deepens him and lives within him like a higher being. To understand and recognize man requires an understanding of his relationship to the Christ Being. And to live earthly life in the right way as a human being requires a proper relationship to the power of Christ. The Christmas Conference speaks of this Christ force:[1]

"At the Turning Point of Time
The Cosmic-Spirit-Light entered

The stream of earthly Evolution;
Darkness of Night
Had ceased to reign;
Day-radiant Light
Shone in the souls of men . . ."

Something that enters mankind from such lofty heights will become more and more a decisive stream, the stream of spirit love in mankind. Over long ages of evolution, through incarnations in many periods of history it will transform man until his higher being has been born "as the Child".

A spiritual stream of transformation such as this, in which the Christ Being is working, must be guided by those who stride ahead of their time; we call them leaders of mankind. The highest teachers of mankind, twelve Bodhisattvas, are gathered around the Christ Being; from supersensible worlds they let flow into mankind what he needs in order to progress. Reflecting higher laws, Christ gathered His twelve disciples, awaking in them the seeds of the future. This awakening of future seeds is expressed, for instance, in the initiation of Lazarus by Christ. Moving among mankind in this way are individualities who have united themselves with the Christ impulse and proceed through history as Christ initiates, working tirelessly for the Spirit of Love, helping man to become mature for this Spirit and his earth mission.

This is a brief indication of what is meant by giving "that which we will" its "proper place in the mission of the earth". Now how did mankind on earth receive and treat the Bringer of Love? Just as His deed was answered by the Crucifixion, that crime out of the forces of darkness, so has every imitation of Christ since then been punished. Persecution, hate, torture, death are the reactions of those "evils which hold sway", who vehemently oppose the mission of the earth. It is human beings who take their place in the battle *against* the mission of the earth in order to prevent the victory of the Spirit of Love. These are the negative images of evolution. All this, both the good and the evil, is expressed in the way the destiny of every life is shaped. We are confronted with the central supersensible motifs of a biography if we can become aware of what forces are rising up from the depths of the subconscious. We come quite close to the core of a human being if we notice that there is a constant inner search going on within him. We could say that his secret is revealed in this search since it is the expression of the most deeply spiritual force in his destiny. The human being seeks his parents, his place of birth, his language, the community within which he will spend his childhood and youth. He seeks his teachers, his friends, his sickness and health, the impulses and conflicts of life, the difficulties of his life and the obstacles these place in his path; he seeks his partner, the one who belongs to his destiny. All this he seeks as his *destiny.* Out of higher laws comes the constellation of his spiritual development in the community of souls in the stream to which he belongs. The reasons lie in former earth lives from which he brings new goals. Deepest spiritual laws lie hidden here according to which we live and which bring about transformation and inner growth, transformation which leads to being more human, and inner growth which we undergo as human beings. In the whole of this process of searching under the guidance of the spirit which gives direction to the human being's life path, just as the compass guides the ship, his relationship to the Christ Being is of paramount importance in his inner development. It is even decisively important that as a child he should be able to absorb the images of the life of Jesus Christ, for they exercise undreamt of forces of awakening in the depths of the soul. In the same way the inner knowing of the human being faces the esoteric truth that the Christ is the being Who lives and works with all His strength within the community of human beings. Where destiny is borne, achieved, experienced, fulfilled and righted in the interweaving of human soul with human soul, the essential ingredient is in reality the acceptance of the Christ impulse. In every individual He becomes the highest impulse. This can never be achieved in solitary withdrawal, for it only rays forth and gains substance when it weaves among men. Noting this weaving among and within human beings we cannot but confess that the Christ himself lives within the destiny laws of human beings.

Rudolf Steiner spoke of all these mysteries of life in many of his lectures. And he himself lived and acted in accordance with them. For instance if we can become absorbed in his lectures on the Gospels and even inwardly hear his words, we sense that he gave all his descriptions out of his own actual seeing of the Mystery of Golgotha and that he lived directly within this Mystery.

The inner struggle with the facts of life as they are today calls for a quite new recognition and understanding of the Mystery of Golgotha. This recognition and understanding on the one hand and a new understanding of human biography on the other often show even in the smallest detail how much this biography has to do with the path of Christ. The link between the two, when understood in this way, is the key to the individual's recognition of himself as a Mystery pupil. This brings us to the often characteristic stamp of the biography of those human beings whose task it is to play a leading role in the spiritual life of mankind. Such biographies encompass an often hidden image slaughtered; when He embarks on the road to crucifixion the disciples sleep and do not understand; when He is hunted and pursued there is a Judas who sees to it that He is captured; when He ought to be defended there is a Peter who knows Him not; when He is innocent before the court He is condemned to death and scourged, and when He dies He is mocked. Yet his bearing and conduct speak the words of love: Forgive them, for they know not what they do.
them, for they know not what they do.

The ego of the human being is his true spiritual being. It stems from the spiritual world, is born of God, and on earth takes hold of a physical body with which it can develop consciousness of its own self in the struggle with earthly gravity and darkness. The more the force of the spirit is awakened in the human being — as perhaps in the Jesus-Zarathustra Individuality — the greater is the spirituality that streams from him, permeating his physical body which is his sheath and his tool on earth. More and more the human being is then permeated by the ego in his deeds and thus also in his biography.

The Christ as the Ego of the Cosmos entered into a human body. This took place during the Baptism in the Jordan in the thirtieth year of Jesus of Nazareth. He was the first being from the lofty divine world, an immortal, Who clothed Himself in a sheath made of earthly material, a mortal body. Through it He experienced the earthly world: its heaviness, its darkness, its separateness from the realms of the heavens and their all-pervading power. This immortal Cosmic Ego learnt to live in a mortal body "like a man", learnt to suffer and to die in feebleness. The Christ Ego entered into the death process and gave it the stamp of life so that death became the true life. That is the event of Golgotha, the mystery of the new dying: resurrection.

What we perceive is true if we see a kinship between the ego of a human being which incarnates into an earthly life and the "Incarnation of a God". Profound links are at work between the human ego and the Christ Ego. The human being who experiences the Christ as a divine archetype for his own development also takes Him into himself as the bringer of peace and love.

One who "places himself within the mission of the earth" is one who works for knowledge of the Christ Ego. He also works for knowledge of the human ego in all its cosmic evolution. And he learns to know and understand the earth as the dwelling place of the Christ Being, Who will transform all the earthly laws of nature from out of the spirit. And with that he finds himself in the midst of Anthroposophy.

These spiritual realities resound in the words spoken by Rudolf Steiner at the Laying of the Foundation Stone: "that that which we will may take its place as a part of that which we feel to be the mission of the earth".

Nine Years after the Laying of the Foundation Stone: The Burning of the Goetheanum

On 31 December 1922, after Rudolf Steiner had finished his New Year's Eve lecture in the Goetheanum, the smell of burning was observed at 10 o'clock. Soon the fire, which was raging in the double wall of the big cupola, was spotted, and at midnight the flames broke through into the dark winter night.

In the report by Heinz Muller[16] important details about this act of destruction are given. Many members have told about the conduct of Rudolf Steiner, about his precise instructions for the fighting of the fire and how during the course of the whole night he kept appearing, now here, now there, watching everything and making observations. It was soon evident that nothing more could be done to contain the fire: the cupola collapsed with a loud roar and flames flared skyward. "Ten years of work" was all Rudolf Steiner said. In the physical world the enemy had accomplished what he had set out to do: the destruction of that Centre which had been founded to further a new relationship to the spiritual world. But he had not counted on the will force, on the fighting power of Rudolf Steiner's spirit: On the morning of the New Year, 1 January 1923 — as if he had not been awake all that night enduring destruction, total ruin and the abyss — Rudolf Steiner continued with the cycle of lectures which he had started before Christmas on the theme of the appearance of natural science in world history and its subsequent development.[17]

In his book *Meetings with Rudolf Steiner*[18] Albert Steffen wrote about the continuation of the work after the fire. "He set us all an example. Nobody who witnessed it can ever forget it. A few days after the ruinous fire he put on a eurythmy performance in the Schreinerei; in spite of the emotional shock and physical fatigue which these days had brought, this was one of the greatest artistic achievements I have ever experienced. An unheard of degree of spiritual freedom and creative virtue must have lived in Rudolf Steiner for him to overcome in such a sublime manner the misfortune intended to destroy him. In order to give strength to his fellow workers and friends, he made visible for them what they had experienced inwardly in that gruesome night. First he made them see the midnight monologue of Faust. Four grey women appear: Imperfection, Guilt, Care and Need — the "Fatal Sisters" of Death, in sackcloth and ashes, moved by the desert wind. Inwardly quaking we heard the words:

'The night seems to penetrate ever more thickly,
In my inmost self alone a light shines clear.
What I have planned, I must complete it quickly,
Only the Master's word is weighty here.'

"Then the colours of decay were replaced by those of becoming. Lighter figures in bluish and reddish robes drove them away.

'The spiritual beauty
Of heavenly children
Passes before
Faltering despair.'

"Everyone who takes Anthroposophy seriously knows that the exercises necessary if one is to penetrate into the supersensible world require that the *soul* be made into an instrument for investigation. One must be able to confront oneself objectively.

"Here far more was done. Here an enormous loss was not only borne without weakening, but was made into a gain in the inner being of others. Rudolf Steiner, whose own work was destroyed, continued to shower gifts on mankind."[18]

All the same, this night had touched the roots of his physical existence, the maintenance of his health forces. He not only continued his arranged schedule, in which there was already hardly a free minute, but even increased his energy and work load in a way that could no longer be measured by human standards. But his furrowed face showed an infinite suffering and a hidden struggle for his physical forces. After the fire he confided to Dr. Ita Wegman that during the fire on New Year's Eve he had had to withdraw for a short while; he had to battle to prevent his own life forces from leaving his body. Since then he had lived only by virtue of the force and power of his higher spiritual members, whereas his physical body as such had become little more than a corpse. Ita Wegman wrote about this in an essay:

"With the destruction of the Goetheanum on the physical plane, the spiritual members of Rudolf Steiner were loosened from his physical body and thus the possibility arose that he too . . . would leave us on this physical plane . . . (And so he remained) as a human being who had his spiritual members completely in the spiritual world whence he merely directed his physical body."[19]

Rudolf Steiner described his condition in a letter of 15 October 1924 to Marie Steiner as follows: "I told you some time ago how since January 1923 the union of the higher members of my being with my physical body has no longer been complete; I lost, as it were, when living in the spiritual realm, the immediate connection with my physical organization. Not with the physical world. On the contrary, the possibility of a sound judgment of the latter became ever stronger and also more comprehensive. But just because in the spiritual world, also for the physical world, everything went along without the slightest confusion, the opponents are trying it with the physical body."[20]

Whereas he expressed himself in those lines as a strictly matter-of-fact observer, he found deeply pained words concerning the fire itself. We know a poem of his which is published in *Wahrspruchworte*":[21]

Nach dem Brand des Goetheanum

Gedanke ward an Gedanken gewunden,
Im Schaffen freudig die Seele verbraucht,
In Formen die Empfindung gehaucht —
Und so der Geist der Kunst verbunden.

Willst du die Schmerzen wohl erkunden
In die das Schicksal uns getaucht?
Gefühl ist in Flammen verraucht,
Schaffensglück hat ein Ende gefunden.

In Trümmer schaut das Auge.

After the Burning of the Goetheanum

Thought was bound to other thought,
Creating with joy our soul worn out,
Feeling breathed into forms about,
And thus the spirit to art was brought.

Willst know the pains which have us caught,
With which our fate has wound us about?
Feeling in smokey flames went out,
To happy creating an end was brought.

The eye sees ruins.

When soon after the fire, in January 1923, Rudolf Steiner was staying in Stuttgart, the members were assembled in the hall in the Landhaus Strasse for a lecture. In complete silence they waited for him; then they heard his steps descending slowly from the top floor to the hall. As he came in, they all rose from their seats and in this way expressed their shared grief and their bonds with him. In the hush he passed through the hall, up the few steps to the platform and to the place where he usually stood for his lectures. The members sat down, and breaking the silence in the room he slowly spoke the sentence: "The Goetheanum in Dornach, under construction for ten years, is no more."[22]

Rudolf Steiner then gave his lecture which was published under the title *Words of grief. A challenge to search our consciences. Words towards the awareness of responsibility.* In a calm and detached way he spoke about the dreadful catastrophe of the fire and about the extent of the grief "for which there are no words". "Perhaps members here (in Stuttgart) will appreciate especially keenly what the Society as a whole has lost in the Building that became its home."[22]

Rudolf Steiner then spoke stern words about the "widespread capacity for illusion in our circles", about the need for a strong, energetic Anthroposophical Society which should stand behind a rebuilding, otherwise it would make no sense. In quite a special way, moreover, our soul should occupy itself at present with the following words which solemnly, as in a hymn, pronounce the being of Anthroposophia; and the soul should ever again return to this spirit-poem. Ten years after the laying of the Foundation Stone in 1913, the link between Anthroposophy and the Being of Love himself is expressed in language born of grief. "After all, the Dornach Building was built through love . . . and indeed, it perished under the sign of love . . . While hatred raged all around (1914-1918), true love prevailed in Dornach and was incorporated into the Building — love that had its origin in the spirit."[22]

These words of truth which spring from a spiritual source are appropriately followed by those below which themselves have a unique position, not only in this lecture, but as words of initiation within the entire work of Rudolf Steiner and which should be recognized as such:

"Ideas are for Anthroposphy
vessels, formed out of love,
into which the being of man, spiritually,
is brought from spiritual worlds.
Clothed in thoughts formed with love
the light of true humanity
shall shine through Anthroposophy.
And knowledge is but the form
in which through man
it shall be possible
that the true spirit from the widths of the world
will focus in human hearts,
that from the hearts of men
it may enlighten human thought.
And as Anthroposphy
really can only be grasped through love,
therefore it is love-creating
if it is grasped by Man in its true being.
Therefore, in the midst of furious hatred
a place of love could be built in Dornach.
And words
will not be coined in the Anthroposophical realm
as they are usually coined today.
Words are formed
that are all intrinsically pleas.
Every word in Anthroposophy
if it is spoken in the right sense
is fundamentally a plea
a reverent plea:
A plea
that the spirit may come down to mankind."[22]

Because there were no words to express the extent of the grief for the loss of the Goetheanum, the words spoken to the members in this lecture hour were born out of the dreadful grief itself. They bear the golden aura of eternal words. They possess the element of love which once, at the Turning Point Of Time, flowed to men through death. They come with the power of speech which is appropriate for the Time Spirit who is the Bringer of the Earth Spirit.

The deed of destruction which was inspired by the Spirit of Darkness was confronted by the Spirit of the Goetheanum, the Spirit of Love. In the words which Rudolf Steiner spoke about the Goetheanum that had been taken away from the physical world, the seeds for the Christmas Conference were already present: "In its visible forms and as a visible work of art, the Goetheanum spoke of the secrets of the spiritual world to an immeasurably greater number of people than had previously been able to learn of them through the spoken word . . . So the Goetheanum became the means of communicating the sacred concern of the Anthroposophical Society even to people who had no interest in the Society as such."[22]

Eleven months after this, on 25 December 1923, the spiritual Foundation Stone for this "sacred concern" was laid in the hearts of members.

The burnt-out ruin of the first Goetheanum

Spiritual Constellations

During the *Christmas Conference 1923*, which took place within the thirteen holy nights, events occurred which require to be studied with an inward eye if their significance is to be noticed and understood. A question may point to an inner connection between a rather more outward event and a spiritual view of the Christmas Conference with which we are concerned here. The question is: *How did Rudolf Steiner mention and treat the Goetheanum during the Christmas Conference?*

In reply to a remark made by Herr van Leer, a friend from Vienna, "You mention the Goetheanum — but we have no Goetheanum!" Rudolf Steiner gave an answer which places the whole matter in a new light and puts a highly spiritual reality in regard to the Goetheanum in the forefront of our attention. He said: "We do not consider that we have no Goetheanum . . . We consider that we have no Building . . . but the Goetheanum itself is still here." — "Is it not important . . . here as everywhere else to stress that for us it is the spiritual which has the greater importance? . . . The Goetheanum is present before our spiritual eyes!"[1]

This decided statement that the *Goetheanum* does exist is borne out by other examples too. Rudolf Steiner speaks of the *Vorstand at the Goetheanum and of the Free High School for Spiritual Science, Goetheanum, Dornach.*

Why is such particular stress placed on this during the Christmas Conference? This question touches on something extraordinary of which the members then were hardly aware. Before the fire, the *Goetheanum* had been neither opened nor *consecrated*. True, the first course of the High School, which had been held in the hall of the Goetheanum, had indeed been opened by a special recitation from the third Mystery Play *The Guardian of the Threshold* of a speech by Hilarius, the Grand Master of the Mystery Brotherhood. Rudolf Steiner had changed the wording for this. The first part is quoted here:

"In that spirit's name who has revealed himself
to many souls in our center of striving,
I now appear before these persons who,
from now on wish to hear the words
that here resound earnestly to the souls.
The powers who guide our progress on the earth
could not, in earlier times,
reveal themselves in a full conscious way.
For it was as with children; gradually
the forces had to be matured and strengthened
that were designed to carry on our knowing.
So was it that mankind in general
had slowly to unfold in course of time.
In darkness lived at first those impulses
that later came to show themselves as worthy
to see the spirit-light from higher worlds.
In those remotest days when earth began,
souls dedicated to the spirit were chosen,
to be the wise and watchful guides of men.
They cultivated in centres of wisdom
those spirit-forces that sent rays of knowledge
into the souls, which only in dim consciousness
could be penetrated by their vision."[21]

But in an address to the members about the High School course he had said earlier:

"In conclusion I wish to announce that on Saturday 25 September, the day before our autumn High School course begins, there will be a meeting here at 8:00 pm for all the members who are at present in Dornach. Anyone who is here on the evening of 25 September should please come so that we can make suitable arrangements and properly 'do the honours' towards all the non-members who are coming to the High School course. Stewards will be appointed who will wear a red rosette in their buttonhole; they will help everyone to find a seat over in the Building, and so on. There will be all sorts of other posts too, not as durable, maybe, as in the outside world, but more honourable in some ways, and so on and so on. We are the ones who must spread civilities in all directions when guests come to us. And so that we can offer every possible courtesy to our guests we shall meet here on Saturday 25 September at 8 o'clock in the evening.

"May I draw your attention to one point, however, so that members do not get a wrong impression which might then lead to bewilderment among the guests from outside: *It is not our Goetheanum, but only our High School course, which will be opened on 26 September. The opening of the Goetheanum lies in the far distant future. The world will have to muster a far more intense understanding of what goes on here if the Goetheanum is truly to be inaugurated one day.* It is only because we have no other room for our High School courses that they will have to be held in the hall over in the Building. We are simply going to use the unfinished Goetheanum as a place in which to hold our High School courses. You will find all the other arrangements listed in the announcements."[23]

Rudolf Steiner's earnest warning to the members "so that members do not get a wrong impression which might lead to bewilderment among the guests from outside: It is not our Goetheanum . . . which will be opened on 26 September . . . The opening of the Goetheanum lies in the far distant future . . ." shows clearly the direction of his thoughts about an opening of the Goetheanum in the sense of a consecration: He was concerned that a precondition for a consecration did not yet exist, namely a spiritual response to the Goetheanum as a Mystery Centre. He discussed this in an essay published on 18 March 1923 in the journal *Das Goetheanum* under the title *The Goetheanum in its first ten years:*

"I now find something that is curiously in harmony with the conception of the Goetheanum Building: that at the time of the first event within the Goetheanum it would have gone very much against the grain with me to have had an opening ceremony for the Goetheanum itself. The programme of that lecture cycle simply was not suitable for a festive ceremony of that kind. This was not to take place until it was possible to arrange a programme that would have been totally in harmony with the original idea of the Building. It never happened. The Goetheanum died away beforehand. Everlasting mourning now dwells in the hearts of those who loved it."[24]

A little later in the same essay he writes: "But though it was not possible for us to celebrate *the* opening ceremony that would have revealed in complete harmony the idea of the Building together with the content of the event in the Goetheanum, nevertheless during the course of over two years a number of attempts were made in various directions to make the spiritual way of Anthroposophy effective . . . At the end of September and beginning of October 1921 a number of German theologians who bore within their souls an impulse for Christian religious renewal gathered at the Goetheanum. The work on this theme was brought to a conclusion in September 1922. What I myself experienced with these theologians in September 1922 was for me one of the festivals of my life. This took place in the small hall in the south wing where later the fire was first was discovered. It was possible here, together with a number of nobly inspired human beings, to tread a path that leads spiritual knowledge into religious experience."[24]

The following passage from a lecture given in London on 25 April 1922 points very clearly to the common life source from which both the supersensible ideas and the forms of the Goetheanum are drawn: "The architectural forms of the Goetheanum are drawn from the very source from which spring the ideas of the supersensible expressed in words. Everything that is found in Dornach, be it sculpture or painting, is carried by a new style out of which Anthroposophy is to be born in this modern age. Whoever visits this Free High School for Spiritual Science will find that on the one hand the anthroposophical world view is proclaimed from the rostrum in words and on the other hand the forms of the Building and the paintings portray in an artistic way what is expressed by the word."[25]

Rudolf Steiner spoke of the destruction of the Goetheanum as a *dying away*. This is an expression that can only be used of something that is alive. A lifeless building cannot *die away*. But since this expression was deliberately chosen it is up to us to generate thoughts about it which tread an entirely unaccustomed path if we are to gain a perception which has hitherto hardly ever been brought into the world of the soul.

The clear and direct conclusion to be drawn from the sentence "the Goetheanum died away beforehand" can be none other than that *it must previously have existed as a living being!* In the spiritual scientific sense this means that an external physical body must have possessed an etheric body. An etheric body is closely linked with everything that lives, including the cosmos. Its laws are connected with the spiritual ether cosmos and when they are brought into the physical world they are also of cosmic nature. *Cosmos* means *beauty*, so all forms directly drawn from the etheric world must therefore reveal a living etheric beauty. The Goetheanum had living forms which reacted to everything that took place within the Building: they accepted or rejected. Rudolf Steiner mentioned this in a number of lectures:

"In Dornach the attempt has been made to take the living principle to the point where the merely dynamic, measured, symmetrical forms of earlier buildings are led over into the organic world . . . the attempt has been made to find a living way into the creative organic principle of nature." (29.6.1921)[26]

"Friends who attended eurythmy performances in the Goetheanum will surely have felt how the architectural forms and decoration of the auditorium harmonized with and responded intimately to the movements of eurythmy. It was even possible to have the feeling that the movements of the performers on the stage there were born of those architectural and plastic forms. If one stood on the podium speaking from the heart out of a truly anthroposophical spirit, every line and form responded and harmonised with what one was saying. That was our goal there . . . That is why those who worked on the Goetheanum at Dornach have the sensation that the very feelings they put into their efforts went up in the flames of New Year's Eve." (27.2.1923)[22]

In the second volume of the Karma Lectures Rudolf Steiner dealt with a quite special effect that emanated from the Goetheanum. On 27 April 1924 he pointed out that mankind today was not receptive to matters of destiny. No thought was given to the events that occur in different ways in a person's life. Yet people had not always been so insensitive about these matters. Comparatively recently people had still sensed that the blows of destiny came from other worlds, including the events of destiny they themselves brought about. — The notable aspect of all this today belongs to an important facet of spiritual scientific psychology; the tendency of people to look out only into nature.

"If a person only looks out into nature all the time, the soul aspect of his sense perceptions deteriorates. He is consumed in his soul through his sense perceptions."[27]

In olden times *temple architecture* was the means of healing the organic damage done to man by looking out merely into nature. This architecture guarded against the consuming of his soul forces through the senses and brought him back to his inner being.

"If you go about with inner knowledge deepened through Imagination, and with sense perceptions made whole and complete through forms created and inspired by a real understanding of man's nature, then your feeling in regard to blows of destiny will be the same as it was in olden times. By cultivating the domain that lies between the experience of true architectural form and the experience of true, symbolic imagery along the path inwards, a man becomes sensitive to the blows of destiny. He feels that what befalls him comes from earlier lives on earth . . .

"But what is of salient importance is that within the Anthroposophical Movement there shall be right thinking. The architecture that would have fulfilled the needs of modern man, that would have been able to capture his gaze in the right way and to lead naturalistic perception, which veils and obscures the vision of karma, gradually into real vision — this architecture did once exist, in a certain form.

And the fact that anthroposophical thoughts were uttered in the setting of those forms, kindled the inner vision. Among its other aspects the Goetheanum Building, together with the way in which Anthroposophy would have been cultivated in it, was in itself an education for the vision of karma. And that is what must be introduced into modern civilization: education for the vision of karma."[27]

In the address with which he welcomed participants to the Christmas course for teachers at the Goetheanum which took place from 23 December 1921 to 7 January 1922, Rudolf Steiner started with the following words of greeting:

"I greet you all most cordially out of the whole spirit and sense of our Movement. Indeed, ladies and gentlemen, it is not a single person who greets you but above all the Building; the Goetheanum itself greets you."[28]

These few remarks by Rudolf Steiner, selected from among many more, give the impression that the Goetheanum was an actual being deserving of respect and reverence. Even in the very first year of the building work, in July 1914, Rudolf Steiner spoke of the mystery of life, the relationship of the Building to the etheric body of the human being. The special etheric sheath which had surrounded the ancient true Mystery Centres was present here from the beginning. We are increasingly filled with the sensation of a deeply hidden etheric union between Building and Master Builder, woven like a protective sheath in order to receive and absorb the highest impulses of a new mystery centre. The destruction by fire, the dying away of this Building must thus have had a deep effect and been a terrible blow to the physical and etheric sheaths of the Master Builder. Only those who sensed the mystery secrets of the Dornach Hill could perceive this.

The destruction of the Goetheanum was not the only attack wrought by the stream that fought stubbornly and ceaselessly against all spiritual knowledge, guided by the forces of darkness. The year which followed the fire, 1923, revealed the disintegration of the Anthroposophical Society. There was no spiritually awake leadership in the Anthroposophical Society capable of shaping Society affairs on a scale that could contain the fullness of anthroposophical spiritual research. Rudolf Steiner as a spiritual researcher and teacher of Anthroposophy had nothing to do with the leadership. During this one year he journeyed from country to country in Europe in order to persuade the national Societies to create for themselves a clearcut form and leadership. This gave him deep insight into the limited abilities of the membership to form themselves consciously into a community.

Community building demands exceptional and wakeful consciousness and calls for a stern discipline with regard to personal self-assertion which so often make the larger tasks impossible to complete. It was necessary to recognize the extent to which community building is inseparable from inner moral schooling.

The painful conclusions he reached led Rudolf Steiner to the decision to found the *General Anthroposophical Society* under his own chairmanship and with its central office at the Goetheanum in Dornach. In this way the building up of the Society as well as its leadership and shaping were taken into the hands of the only one capable of carrying out the task in accordance with the conditions arising from the spiritual world. Thus there was from the beginning an intimate congruence and harmony between the being of Anthroposophy and the earthly form of the Society. The form itself was therefore Anthroposophy. It might be said that at the Christmas Conference in Dornach, when the spiritual Foundation Stone of the Anthroposophical Society was laid, an incarnation of the spiritual being Anthroposophy into the body of the Society was brought about.

In the shaping of the Goetheanum Building Rudolf Steiner always had in mind the creation of a living and artistic form filled with organic movement, a form which expressed itself in the Building through its own life forces, like a being. Between the spirit of the Building and its external manifestation there is a relationship like that between a nut and its shell: the outer part arises out of the nature of the inner part. Indeed, comparison with man himself is equally possible: the *spiritual individuality* of the human being, his kernel, creates in its outer form an *architectural and living sheath* for its being, like a *nutshell.*

Having created a Building out of the principle of the inner spirit that revealed in a unique way the harmony between inner and outer aspects, how was the architect to set about the new task of forming a *Society of Anthroposophy* in which the same archetypal principle of creation would also be the determining factor? How was the being of *Anthroposophy* itself to tell him that it desired a *Society* with forms in which it could live purposefully and creatively without any frustrations from rigidifid formalities, bureaucracy or the platitudes of ordinary societies?

Rudolf Steiner sought a solution without any spiritual compromise: On the one hand he created a form clearly delineating the competence and structure of the leadership; on the other hand he always endeavoured to run the Society's day to day affairs in a lively spiritual way *without any red tape.* "It was necessary to break away from anything that might smack of the traditional way of running society affairs" and "Voting in the Anthroposophical Society is an impossibility," were his definitive formulations. The spiritual aim at the Christmas Conference was to fuse into a unity the spiritual kernel of Anthroposophy with the form of the Society, or to encompass all the members in one *Anthroposophical Society.* This unity was and has remained the existential problem of the Society. Concealed within it is the task as such of the leadership of mankind as a whole.

Let us remember that in the ancient Lemurian age of earthly man's development the human physical body was rendered so tough, rigid and immobile that it became a useless shell for the souls of that time. So they withdrew to other parts of the cosmos, to the various planets where they waited to see whether soft, pliable bodies would once again become available for incarnation on earth. This was indeed brought about by the extrication of the moon from the earth, the bearer of the hardening impulse in the physical, and its banishment to an orbit around the earth which would prevent any more disturbance of the development tasks of mankind. This grand cosmic process, therapy on a universal scale, has remained like an archetypal image countering the tendency or danger of any hardening process. We can sense how in the formation of the Anthroposophical Society everything was tackled that might have led to the sheath becoming unfit to absorb or serve spiritual impulses. Everything was done and planted in the souls and hearts of the members to ensure that they should be able to absorb the spiritual, to absorb the Anthroposophical Movement. To this end Rudolf Steiner spoke most essential words in his opening address on 24 December 1923, to be unforgettably imprinted in the depths of souls:

"Not from an earthly arbitrary choice, but in obedience to the call sounding forth from the spiritual world, — not from an earthly arbitrary choice, but in view of the sublime pictures which arose out of the spiritual world as the modern revelation of the spiritual life of humanity, the impulse sprang for the Anthroposophical Movement. This Anthroposophical Movement is not an earthly service; this Movement is, in its entirety, in all particulars, a service of the gods, a divine service . . .

"We intend to pick up the thread at the point where we would so gladly have picked it up in 1913.[29] Let us pick it up again, and let us inscribe in our souls as the highest principle for the Anthroposophical Movement, which shall have the Anthroposophical Society as its vehicle: Everything in this Movement *is willed by the spirit,* it wills to be fulfillment of what the signs of the times reveal in shining letters to the hearts of men. Only when we are thus able to make the Anthroposophical Movement in ourselves the deepest concern of the heart will the Anthroposophical Society endure. If we cannot do this it will not continue its existence . . .

"I want you to be aware that if this gathering takes its course in the right way, if this gathering can become thoroughly conscious of how the spiritual esoteric element alone must be the foundation of all our working and being, then those spiritual seeds, which are present everywhere, will be able to germinate, warmed by your mood and your enthusiasm.

"My dear friends, prepare your souls that they may take in these seeds; for your souls are the right soil for the germination, unfolding and development of these spirit seeds. And they are the truth."[1]

Indeed, with the following sentence he approached a particular secret of Dornach even more closely: "Everywhere out of the *spiritual* content of the Anthroposophical Movement warmth seems to come towards us, a warmth that can breathe life into countless seeds which the very soil of Dornach and all that belongs to it holds hidden for the spiritual life of the future.[1]

So how could an anthroposophical community be built which would be a *Goetheanum* transposed into spirit and soul? As an answer to this question we have before us the creation and process of the Christmas Conference. The spirit guiding it and, acting as a cosmic artist-being, bringing about this new *social* creation, this spirit would be the Spirit of the Goetheanum, the Spirit of the new Mysteries.

We are not dealing here with a mere analogy, a similarity between the Goetheanum Building and the Anthroposophical Society. The connection between the Goetheanum and the whole treatment, execution and substance of the *Christmas Conference* is founded on an infinitely profound and moving spiritual reality. This reality must be contemplated with inner eyes so powerfully that it fills the spirit with the vision of how the invisible works in the world.

On the evening of 1 January 1924 Rudolf Steiner spoke of the stream of spiritual reality:

"For it is true that the impulse that properly permeates what must now stream forth from Dornach must be one springing not from the earth but from the spiritual world. I have emphasized this from all sorts of angles during the last few days. We must develop the strength to follow impulses from the spiritual world."[1]

Then he returned once again to the request with which he had opened the Conference on 24 December; on the ninth day he emphasized this once more:

"More important than anything else we take away with us will be the mood we take with us, the mood for the spiritual world, giving us the certainty that in Dornach a central point for spiritual knowledge will be created."[1]

At the end of the Conference a member gave voice to the heartfelt gratitude of all those present: "We owe to the one who spoke to us this evening nothing less than the joy of our spiritual life . . . " Rudolf Steiner's answer to this was couched in all-encompassing words about the Spirit of the Goetheanum:

"I know that I was permitted to say what took place here for it was said with full responsibility *with eyes raised to the Spirit who is and will be the Spirit of the Goetheanum.* In his name over the past few days I have permitted myself to speak words which would not have been so strongly formulated if they had not been spoken with eyes raised to the Spirit of the Goetheanum, to the good Spirit of the Goetheanum. So let me accept these thanks in the name of the Spirit of the Goetheanum for whom we will work and strive in the world."[1]

The Spirit of the Goetheanum! How substantially real these words make him! Every detail of what Rudolf Steiner himself saw can be heard in these sentences! And what was this? He himself led us to the "Spirit of the Goetheanum" when on New Year's Eve during the Christmas Conference he spoke of the connection between the burning of the Temple of Ephesus (356 BC) and the burning of the Goetheanum:

"In Ephesus the statue of the God; here in the Goetheanum the statue of Man, the statue of the Representative of mankind, Christ Jesus. In Him, identifying ourselves in all humility with Him, we seek to attain to knowledge, even as once in their way, a way that is no longer fully understood by mankind today, the pupils of Ephesus attained to knowledge in Diana of Ephesus."[1] "For one sensitive to such things there was indeed in this Goetheanum a memory of the Temple of Ephesus."[1]

The evening then closed with a resolve solemnly formulated by Rudolf Steiner who was now the Chairman, since the Anthroposophical Movement had become identical with the Anthroposophical Society:

"We shall only become worthy through the task which has been laid upon us, since we have been permitted to build this Goetheanum, if today in memory we resolve, each before the best and most divine within our soul, to remain true to the spiritual impulses which were given a form in that Goetheanum. That Goetheanum could be taken from us. If we remain truly honest and upright in our will, the Spirit of the Goetheanum cannot be taken from us."[1]

In each deeply moved inner being this resolve of faithfulness became an unbreakable vow of faithfulness to Rudolf Steiner and the *Goetheanum*. This pledge of faithfulness above all else was the firm rock; it lived unswervingly in the personalities who comprised the founding Vorstand around Rudolf Steiner; it lived unswervingly in their fulfillment of their tasks.

Someone who in later years might presume to maintain that the Christmas Conference did not succeed cannot possibly have known anything about this moment of initiation with its resolve to faithfulness. Many held absolutely firmly to it for the rest of their lives. And one above all others never wavered, one who stood within the pledge together with the others — Rudolf Steiner.

The Supersensible Aspect of the Christmas Conference

Dealing with the Christmas Conference in depth, dwelling on and contemplating every part of the process and in particular every address given by Rudolf Steiner during the nine founding days, leaves us with impressions which gradually coalesce as the years go by; eventually our soul is faced with a picture of the event which can hardly be comprehended. Thus every comment made about the Conference at the time is an expression of what can only have been a limited understanding. It is always possible to progress to a greater and more mature comprehension.

The programme laying out the sequence of the Conference was headed *Foundation Gathering*. The heading for the second day, 25 December, was: *Laying of the Foundation Stone of the International Anthroposophical Society by Dr. Rudolf Steiner*. Whas was this *Laying of the Foundation Stone* and with it the *Foundation Gathering*? From the very first moment the Conference was a purely spiritual event: The *Foundation Stone* was a three-part meditation on the being of man with a view to the Turning Point Of Time. The Foundation Stone verses were heard supersensibly and received out of the cosmic word. The soil into which the *Foundation Stone* was laid was formed from the hearts of those present. The soil needed for the laying of the Foundation Stone consisted of hearts in harmonious collaboration, hearts with the will, permeated by love, to carry anthroposophical willing through the world.

The dodecahedral Foundation Stone is formed "in this moment" in our souls out of three forces: the Spirit of the heights, the Christ Force of the circumference and the Father Power from the depths.

The Foundation Stone words are spoken "with the will of the spiritual world".

The substance of the Foundation Stone is cosmic human love, the form of the Foundation Stone is cosmic human Imagination, the radiance of the Foundation Stone is cosmic human thought.

The atmosphere in the over-filled Schreinerei during that winter season consisted of heart forces warming everything through and through, of great inner contemplative forces, of all-permeating enthusiasm, of iron-hard decisiveness, and of energetic will to persevere. It was the warmth cosmos of a new beginning, a new *Saturn*.

The spiritual beings who took into themselves in purely spiritual form the deeds of the ceremony were the *egos of the human beings* who were present. These egos raised themselves into the sphere of the Spirit Self and entered into an unbreakable bond of destiny with the Anthroposophical Movement which was present in their midst.

The *Spiritual Goetheanum* was present in new cosmic power of experience.

"Michael desires in the future to set up his abode in the hearts and souls of earthly human beings"[30] said Rudolf Steiner later. Here it had become reality.

And another remark, made before the Christmas Conference, was also realized: "Because the visible sign (the Goetheanum) no longer exists, we must all the more devote ourselves to grasping the inner forces and the inner nature of being of the Anthroposophical Movement and all that belongs to it for the entire development of mankind."[31]

In a way never experienced before, something happened in the makeshift, scanty surroundings of the Schreinerei, something which Rudolf Steiner described on 27 February 1923 as though previewing the events of the Christmas to come:

". . . when, infusing living power into the spiritual ideas we form, we put ourselves in a position actually to experience something of that awakening element, something that does not stop at idealizing our sense experience, leaving it at the stage of an abstract thought, but that endows the ideal with a higher life as we live into it and make it the counterpart of the cultus by raising it from the physical to the supersensible level. We can achieve it in our life of feeling by taking care to imbue everything we do for Anthroposophy with thoroughly spiritualized feeling. We do this when, for instance, we feel that the very doorway we reverently enter on our way to an anthroposophical assemblage is consecrated by the common anthroposophical purpose being served in the room it leads to, no matter how mundane the setting."[22]

We must inwardly experience "that we do not just sit in a room where Anthroposophy is being pursued, a group of so and so many individuals taking in what is being read or spoken and having our own thoughts about it. A real spiritual being must be present in a room where Anthroposophy is being carried on . . . Our hearts and souls and attitudes must learn similarly to invoke the presence of a real spiritual being in a room where Anthroposophy is being talked of . . . that we can feel a real spiritual being hovering there above us looking on and listening. We should divine a supersensible presence, invoked by our pursuit of Anthroposophy."[22]

When we have sufficiently understood all these incisive words spoken by Rudolf Steiner characterising spiritual realities, words which we have here quoted in the context of the Christmas Conference, we begin to discern that they are spiritual pointers to the paths hinted at by the Christmas Conference as a true event in the destiny of mankind. During the course of these nine days something occurred in the Schreinerei which took place from start to finish in the spiritual world. The *Christmas Conference* took place beyond the threshold. In their mood of soul borne by enthusiasm and warmth of heart all the participants experienced a spiritual fulfilment which lent wings to their souls, enabling them to undergo the experience to which Rudolf Steiner had in earlier years pointed as the sign of our times: that mankind should step over the threshold, pass by the Guardian and enter the spiritual world. During those nine days under the guidance of Rudolf Steiner the eight hundred people present experienced the spiritual world in full consciousness in the sense of the *inverted cultus* which raised their souls to the supersensible realm; they entirely absorbed the spiritual world and this experience was firmly bound up in all their subsequent anthroposophical work and striving.

The Christmas Conference made Dornach, made the *Goetheanum* the focal point of the Anthroposophical Society. If the Goetheanum had still stood, these days of highest spiritual consecration would have been *its* consecration. This Goetheanum participated in so comprehensive a manner in the supersensibly real events of those nine days that a kind of mystery consecration streamed from it. And Rudolf Steiner, the master builder, first of a physical Building and now of a spiritual Building of Mankind, was no longer the one he had been hitherto. Out of inner observation of his spiritual path it is permissible to say that he had gained a *rank* higher than any so far attained by a leader of mankind. In independent spiritual sovereignty he undertook two tasks. In earlier cultural epochs two such tasks had never been linked together: the laws of the spiritual world, sternly guarded by Michael, never permitted these two tasks to run parallel with one another because they were mutually exclusive. It had not been possible before to be a researcher into the spirit and at the same time a bearer of earthly responsibilities. When Rudolf Steiner was faced with the inexorable necessity of fully taking on the two tasks he could, as he himself said, only do so by making a vow to the spiritual world. To make this quite clear it is necessary to quote his very words. We find what he said to the members about this in a lecture he gave in Torquay on 12 August 1924:

"The whole basis of the Anthroposophical Movement is that revelations of the substance of spiritual knowledge flow down from the spiritual world. If one wishes to carry out the work of the Anthroposophical Movement, it is not possible to devote oneself exclusively to human affairs and activities. One must be open to receive what may flow from the spiritual worlds. The laws of the spiritual world are definite and inviolable; they must be strictly obeyed. And it is difficult to combine the demands of an external office today — even though it be the Chairmanship of the Anthroposophical Society — with the occult duties connected with the revelations coming from the spiritual world . . . It was necessary to face the possibility that the spiritual powers might have said: This must not be; that there must be no assumption of any external, official position."[32]

It is noticeable that Rudolf Steiner quite emphatically stresses one particular characteristic of the *Dornach Vorstand:* He calls it a *Vorstand of initiative*. This description has caused much puzzlement and conjecture over the years, right down to the objection that surely any member can have initiatives, not only the Goetheanum Vorstand. This manner of thinking obviously fails to grasp the special problem arising out of the fact that the Dornach Vorstand is an *esoteric* Vorstand. To be esoteric necessitates an attitude of soul which quite obviously every person must acquire who strives to conduct his inner development consciously, bringing it into a relationship with the spiritual world. Such a one takes his cue from the laws of the supersensible world and the resulting rules for a proper way of life. In the same way an *esoteric Vorstand* must act in accordance with the relationships and insights which result from its position within the spiritual stream of the *Anthroposophical Movement*. It must ceaselessly ensure that everything that arises in the *Society* by way of institutions, work, activities, tasks and so on is in full harmony with the spiritual world. This connection produces as a matter of course an "esoteric attitude", a spiritual esoteric responsibility. Under Rudolf Steiner this was perfectly natural. It could not possibly have been otherwise.

The nature of initiative is closely linked with this. In a society such as the Anthroposophical Society every aim and every venture must be born primarily out of spiritual impulses. In harmony with what the spirit of the age requires for the development of mankind, "initiative" must permeate all action, striving and realization coming from the inmost centre of the spiritual leadership. No demands and no impulses arising in the external world can constitute determining factors.

The spiritual source for true freedom is the place for impulses and the stimulus for action. Therefore everything connected with a mystery centre must be free from the demands made by any external culture, science or social situation. These are the matters we should turn over in our thoughts if we want to reach an understanding of what is meant by a "Vorstand of initiative". The total scope of this term can only be grasped in connection with the spiritual characteristics with which Rudolf Steiner endowed the "Constitution of the Anthroposophical Society". This is why he was so eager for the development of a special soul capacity related to that of living understanding, namely the power of insight. The Vorstand he formed stood centrally in the midst of spiritual tasks, spiritual leadership and the observance of spiritual laws. Because of this it had to avoid spending all its creative forces on merely administrative matters and guidance of circumstances arising from outside, in order to prevent the setting in of a kind of paralysis of the inner faculties. Therefore Rudolf Steiner placed the work of the Vorstand within two new soul qualities which were to be brought to it by the membership and which were linked to the element of free action and good will: insight and trust.

If the relationship between membership and leadership of the Society is of this quality, then the social unit they comprise will be most permeable and open for spiritual stimulus and purpose. Supported from within in this way the characteristics of a society can unfold and flourish.

What was the vow made to the spiritual world when the spiritual researcher took on the task of society leader or chairman? He had to vow that earthly personal cares, worries, and duties with all their accompanying disharmony, disagreement and dissension would never be carried over into the spiritual world. Everything he did, everything he suggested or gave to people would have to accord fully with the will and impulses of the spiritual world and mirror its dignity and its laws. The spiritual researcher had to take full responsibility for shielding the spiritual world from everything earthly, destructive or hampering. Rudolf Steiner spoke about this at length in a memorial address for his colleague Edith Maryon:

"It is not easy to act responsibly within the Anthroposophical Movement . . . Since the Christmas Conference I have repeatedly had to point out what is stipulated for the leader of the Anthroposophical Movement. It is stipulated that I myself must be able to take what occurs in connection with myself and carry it up into the spiritual world in order to fulfil not only a responsibility towards whatever is here on the physical plane but also a responsibility which reaches up into the spiritual worlds. If you really want to share in what the Anthroposophical Movement has become since the Christmas Conference, you will not be able to avoid entering into a consideration of what it means to be responsible to the spiritual world for the Anthroposophical Movement.

"Something personal that one may stand for on earth if mingled with higher matters, especially those concerning the Anthroposophical Cause, cannot, if it remains personal, be answered for towards the spiritual world. Tremendous problems arise for the one who has to be responsible to the spiritual world for something if he is forced also to answer for what comes out of the personal aspirations of the other participants. You really ought to be a bit aware of the effect this has. The most appalling set-backs are sent out of the spiritual world to the one who attempts to approach it as follows:

"Some person works for the Anthroposophical Movement . . . but in the work he does he mingles personal ambitions, personal intentions and personal qualities. So now we have these personal intentions and tendencies. Most people do not know that they are personal. Most regard what they do as impersonal because they delude themselves as to what is personal or impersonal. Then it has to be taken to the spiritual world with everything else. And this leads to appalling set-backs from the spiritual world for the one who has had to bear these matters, springing up out of the personal realm, into the spiritual world."[33]

All the more moving, indeed shattering, was the communication to the members in his lecture in England (Torquay) on 12 August 1924: "But today it can truly be said, before all the spiritual powers connected with the Anthroposophical Movement, that the links between the spiritual worlds and the revelations which should flow through the Anthroposophical Movement have become more intimate still and the revelations have been vouchsafed in even greater abundance than before; so of the two eventualities, the fortunate one for the progress of the Movement has actually come about. It may now be said that ever since the founding of the Anthroposophical Society at the

Goetheanum those spiritual powers from whom our revelations are received look down upon us with even greater benevolence than before. Therefore in this respect a heavy care has been removed from the Anthroposophical Society."[32]

Rudolf Steiner spoke openly to members about matters which belonged to the most intimate processes of his own development as a result of his position as Chairman of the Society. There were grave consequences in face of the spiritual world which were included in his decision to take over the chairmanship. When he made it conditional at the Christmas Conference that the members at the Foundation Meeting should give their consent, these intimate processes ceased to be his private affair and became the concern of the Society as a whole. The whole Society would have to share the burden of all these cares and possibilities and take them in in full consciousness. Some realities, however, were neither seen nor experienced because the necessary depth and conscious awareness had not yet come about.

To that is added the fact that Rudolf Steiner had attained so high a degree of spiritual development that its significance for the future of the Goetheanum as a new Mystery Centre was and still is incalculable. Earlier on he had quite definitely reckoned with the possibility of living to a great age. He would then have continued to develop his degree of spirituality and would have sent forth from the Goetheanum unimaginably powerful and intensive impulses for cultural renewal.

Something else of which the membership was not fully aware was the relentless and terrible enmity and danger which permanently threatened and surrounded Rudolf Steiner personally. It seemed as though the burning torch that had ignited the Goetheanum, bringing about its destruction, had almost been forgotten. Though Rudolf Steiner spoke of the *dying away* of the Goetheanum, *murder* would have been a more appropriate expression. This would have lit up the murky and evil stream working against the spiritual movement which Rudolf Steiner bore and with which he identified himself.

But as he did not wish the matter to be spoken of as arson, those who knew the truth about this gradually fell silent. However, the knowledge that the Goetheanum had indeed been willfully destroyed by fire was not entirely lost and mention was made of this fact from time to time, even in open publications.[34]

The attempt had been made to destroy the spiritual impulse of Anthroposophy by burning down the home in which it worked, the Free High School for Spiritual Science. If this had been the only attack, then the blow could have been overcome through increased activity and great sacrifice. After the fire Rudolf Steiner quoted a friend who had said to him "If there is something more powerful than destiny, this must be the human being who bears destiny unshaken."

The opposing forces intended, however, to cause such heavy and lasting damage as to make it impossible for any more work on the anthroposophical impulse to be done in the future. So their destructive blows continued.

Rudolf Steiner's health had been severely damaged by the experience of the fire. And yet he compensated for the loss caused by the fire with increased spiritual efforts. So the paralysis of the anthroposophical stream had not been achieved. Indeed the opposite was the case as Anthroposophy continued to spread.

So the strongest attack would have to be against him personally. His physical sheath, that vulnerable mortal body, would have to be the target. And thus it came about.

In her Foreword to the book *Die Weihnachtstagung zur Begründung der Allgemeinen Anthroposophischen Gesellschaft 1923/24* Marie Steiner wrote tellingly about the Conference: "At first all of those who participated in the Conference were lifted out of themselves; they were warmed inwardly through and through and at the same time deeply shaken. But a destiny presided over the whole affair which had to be carried out in another sphere of existence. The consequence has shown what it meant for Dr. Steiner to take our karma upon himself . . . Our human and our Society karma burst upon him with full force immediately after the close of the Christmas Conference. On the last day, 1 January 1924, he fell suddenly and violently ill. As though struck by a sword his life was attacked at a social gathering during which tea and cakes were served, described as a 'Rout' on the programme."'[35]

This Foreword was written in 1944. It is borne out by the following extract from the Postscript[3] she wrote to Rudolf Steiner's autobiography *The Course of my Life.*

"Here the life story ends abruptly. On 30 March 1925, Rudolf Steiner passed away.

"His life, consecrated wholly to the sacrificial service of mankind, was requited with unspeakable hostility; his path of knowledge was transformed into a path of thorns. But he walked the whole way, and mastered it for all mankind. He broke through the limits of knowledge; they are no longer there. Before us lies this path of knowledge in the crystal clarity of thoughts of which this book itself affords evidence. He raised the human intellect up to the spirit, permeated and united it with the spiritual being of the cosmos. In this he achieved the greatest human deed. He taught us to understand the greatest divine deed; he achieved the greatest human deed. How could he escape being hated with all the demonic power of which hell is capable?

"But he repaid with love the lack of understanding with which he was confronted.

"He died — a Sufferer, a Leader, an Achiever —
In such a world as trod him under foot,
Yet which to raise aloft his strength sufficed.
He lifted men; they hurled themselves against him,
They spewed forth hatred, blocked his forward way.
His work they shattered even as he wrought it.
They raged with poison and with flame,
And now with joy defile his memory:

'So he is dead who led you into freedom,
To light, to consciousness, to comprehension

Of what is Godlike in the human soul,
To your own ego, to the Christ.

'Was this not criminal, this undertaking?
He did what once Prometheus expiated,
What gave to Socrates the poisoned cup —
The crime Barabbas wrought was not so vile —
A deed whose expiation is the cross:
He lived, himself, the future there before you.

'We demons cannot suffer such a thing.
We harry, hunt, pursue who dares such deeds,
With all those souls who give themselves to us,
With all those forces which obey our will.
For ours is the turning point of time
And ours this humanity which sickens,
Without its God, in weakness, vice, and error.
We never yield the booty we have won,
But tear to pieces him who dares such deeds.' "

The sudden serious illness which Marie Steiner tells us befell Rudolf Steiner at the tea party on the afternoon of 1 January 1924 came over him with full force just after he had eaten a morsel of cake. White in the face he rose and tottered behind the blue curtain in the Schreinerei hall where he collapsed into the arms of a eurythmist. He called for water which he drank in large amounts and then immediately gave back. This happened several times. Marie Steiner, having suspected that something was the matter, came and had him carried to her little room behind the stage. Then she hurried to find the physician, Dr. Ita Wegman. Rudolf Steiner made strenuous efforts to master the poison and out of the limitless forces of his spirit he succeeded. Slowly he regained control of his body and requested the few witnesses of this incident not to speak further of it. And that same evening he gave one of his most powerful lectures bringing the whole conference to a close and dealing with the theme of passing by the Guardian of the Threshold. Who would have guessed that only a few hours earlier he had himself passed close to death?

From then on he gathered the highest knowledge from the spiritual world: He founded the Michael School at the Goetheanum and gave to this School the indications about the esoteric path to the Guardian of the Threshold. With the speed of winged flight and with irresistible spiritual power he continued to build the impulses of the Christmas Conference, as though spiritual powers were breaking through into the dying cultural life of society. There seemed to be no sleep, no pause, no more adherence to earthly laws for him, as though what he had achieved so far had to be superceded many times over, as though time was too short for him to fulfil the excessive number of tasks awaiting him.

For many the spiritual greatness of Rudolf Steiner at that time became daily more incomprehensible while the path he trod became the greatest riddle surrounding a human being who was, after all, one of our contemporaries, someone we had known for a long time. What was the purpose of this spiritual warrior, this guide and friend of men, a leader on their path, this inexorable and feared opponent of every attempt by ahrimanic and luciferic spiritual temptation to spread darkness? His purpose was at last to carry out on earth a resolve he had been making in spirit for over a thousand years: to bring to completion the greatest spiritual council of mankind that would have immeasurable influence right up into the heights of the spiritual world and into the far distant future. This was *the Christmas Conference in Dornach as the spiritual council of free knowledge.*

Even to approach an understanding of the historical dimensions of Rudolf Steiner's work on earth it will be necessary to probe the depths of the spiritual stream of Michael and the embittered battles fought over it. Once again our attention is drawn to the Goetheanum and its Spirit "who is, who was and who will be", who worked in Rudolf Steiner and was united with him.

Culmination and Sacrifice

What Rudolf Steiner still accomplished after the Christmas Conference was a spiritual culmination of his work. He seemed to be enveloped in the aura of the spiritual supersensible world itself, and all those who had anything to do with him were similarly enveloped and uplifted by this. The whole of the Anthroposophical Society was transformed, almost overnight. Suddenly every word Rudolf Steiner spoke was listened to and his suggestions were carried out with the utmost seriousness coupled with unlimited devotion; it was all so different from the earlier days when the personal ambition and self-assertion of many a member had built up obstacles to spiritual development. Without allowing himself to be deterred by the smear campaign mounted over a wide area by people as well as the churches against his work, the Goetheanum, he calmly and clearly set about taking the necessary steps to rebuild it. The will of the whole Society was united in the goal of building the second Goetheanum. Even during the final part of the Christmas Conference, on that fateful New Year's Day, he drew on the blackboard the archetypal motif on which the forms of the new Goetheanum were to be based. In her book *An die Freunde* in the chapter *Das alte und das neue Goetheanum* Ita Wegman describes how the model came into being:

"He worked feverishly, without any real rest in between. I was allowed to be present and share with astonishment and reverent diffidence the experience of watching the model take shape. After three days it was finished. There is stood, unique in its stern, powerful and yet beautiful forms. And from this model we were now to build the new Goetheanum on the Dornach Hill, a Building for Anthroposophy in the present and future! Anthroposophy with its friends and its opponents needs a Building that does justice to both: In the rooms within we must be able to practise art and hear the word proclaimed by Anthroposophy while on the outside the forms and materials show in their capacity for resistance that it will stand firm and protect what is within.

"Michael Fortress, new Goetheanum.

"Joyfully the master stood beside his model. And after it had been taken from the workshop to the Glass House, where the plans were being drawn, he said to me: 'It caused a sensation when the model was carried from the workshop to its second place of work, the Glass House.' Indeed, how can it do other than cause a sensation when miracles occur before the very eyes of human beings!"[19]

From 8 to 11 April 1924 the great education conference organized by the Vorstand at the Goetheanum together with the College of Teachers of the Waldorf School took place in Stuttgart. A hitherto unsurpassed audience of 1700 gathered to hear the five lectures later published under the title *The Essentials of Education*[36]. It is necessary to mention these lectures for a particular reason. The cordial, elevated, warmly festive mood intensifed from one lecture to the next till in the last it reached a culmination never experienced before. At the end of this lecture Rudolf Steiner gave the final meditation, the new motto of education. After he had proclaimed it in a firm voice in an attitude of holy earnestness towards the task of education there were several minutes of absolute silence in which it would have been possible to hear a pin drop.

"To bind the self to matter
Means to annihilate souls.

To find the self in spirit
Means to unite mankind.

To behold the self in man
Means to build worlds."

Then the audience rose from their seats and the applause and cheering in the hall swelled to a seemingly endless ovation. Rudolf Steiner had to return to the platform again and again and, much moved, waved cordially to the enthused crowd with both hands. This conclusion to the conference was an unforgettable experience. Rudolf Steiner had been recognized.

An extraordinary mood had surrounded these public lectures. It resembled that of the Christmas Conference because by the way they experienced the lectures in spirit the participants had raised themselves to cross the threshold.

With this climax in the revelation of the true spiritual knowledge of man Rudolf Steiner took leave of his work among the wider public. Now he devoted all his strength to making the last few steps into the Mysteries of the present time. He revealed to us the laws and interconnections of destiny, showing us how the laws of karma work among mankind, in history and in individual biographies. The revelation of the laws of karma was his actual spiritual assignment. He commenced six weeks after the Christmas Conference, on 16 February 1924. The spirit of the Christmas Conference was broadened and also, in a specific direction, deepened by the series of lectures on karma. Together with the institution of the Michael School at the Goetheanum, all the lectures Rudolf Steiner gave after the Christmas Conference merged to form a spiritual guidance for the Society, raising it up into an entirely esoteric stream. This spiritual stream was, as Rudolf Steiner put it, desired by the members.

In the way he spoke about the spiritual background to the events of human history one sensed how much more directly he was able to express such things than had been the case formerly. In the fourth lecture of the cycle *The Easter Festival in Relation to the Mysteries* (22.4.1924) the secret of the Goetheanum fire was shown to have its place among the karma of the Mysteries. In this lecture he spoke directly of links with former and present Mystery matters in a way that had not been possible earlier.

"All the spiritual life that passed through the world and evolved through mankind proceeded in ancient times from the Mysteries. The Mysteries were very powerful with respect to the entire guidance of the spiritual life.

"Now mankind was predestined from the outset to evolve spiritual freedom. The development of freedom necessarily involved a decline in the ancient Mysteries. For a period of time human beings had to be less connected with such a mighty guidance as proceeded from the Mysteries; they had to be left more to their own resources . . . A sufficient number of human beings have passed through incarnations in which the power of the Mysteries was felt less than in former ages. And though the fruits of these incarnations are not yet ripe today, though the harvest is not yet, nevertheless it is there within the human beings, it is latent in their souls . . . But this above all will be necessary, that the knowledge, the vision, the conscious experience of the Spiritual that can arise from present-day initiation shall be met, out of the very freedom which men have gained, with reverence and true respect. For if we do not revere, if we do not treasure it, true knowledge or indeed any spiritual life of mankind is in reality impossible."[37]

With these words Rudolf Steiner laid the foundation and also spoke to the deep germinating forces in the souls of those present, showing them how to receive in an attitude of reverence what he had to tell them about the esoteric stream that was to run through the Society. Then he drew their attention to the special nature of present-day Mystery matters:

"It is indeed the case that when that spiritual impulse which has gone forth from here, from the Goetheanum through the Christmas Conference, really finds its way into the life of the Anthroposophical Society" — by bringing about an ever greater depth of understanding — then "this Anthroposophical Society will provide the foundation for the Mysteries of the future. The future life of the Mysteries must consciously be cultivated by this Anthroposophical Society. For this Anthroposophical Society has ever before it an event which can be turned to good account in future evolution even as a similar event was turned to good account once upon a time, namely the burning of the

Temple of Ephesus. Then and now, a great and deep wrong was done. Yet on the different planes of life these things appear in different ways and it lies in the freedom of mankind to turn to good account something that on one plane is a dreadful wrong, for it is just through these terrible events that a real progress of mankind can be achieved."[37]

Having indicated the link between the burning of the Temple of Ephesus and the burning of the Goetheanum, he entered more deeply into the initiation teaching of Ephesus. At that time the most important knowledge was that of the creating of the etheric body before the birth of the human being, "the clothing of the human being in the etheric body", as he puts it. Also important was the experience of the way the many planets worked together in this: Sun — Moon — Mars — Mercury — Jupiter — Venus — Saturn. Two of the initiates participating in these Diana Mysteries at Ephesus were mentioned by Rudolf Steiner during the Christmas Conference as having been the souls who later reincarnated as Aristotle and Alexander. In their Greek incarnation they once more made contact with the Mysteries as they were then cultivated at Samothrace. "Through the influence of the Mysteries of the Kabiri there arose for both of them something like a memory of the old Ephesian time."[37]

In this Easter lecture Rudolf Steiner pointed out the spiritual path to the historical karmic link between the fire catastrophe of Ephesus and that of Dornach. The most important aspect was described as the carrying out into the wide spaces of the cosmic ether of the mystery events of Ephesus. The "continuous Easter festival at Ephesus" that had been "contained within the Temple spaces" was spread abroad and inscribed "into the great dome of the heavens, inasmuch as the heavens are etheric."[37]

Indeed, even in the lectures he gave four weeks before the Christmas Conference in November/December 1923 under the title *Mysteriengestaltungen,* Rudolf Steiner spoke in detail about the burning of the Goetheanum: "Let us look through these flames to those others which once devoured the Temple of Ephesus. And let us take this as a challenge to develop a sense for discovering what lies in the beginning of the Gospel of John. Challenged by these painful holy impulses, let us look back from the Gospel of John to the Temple of Ephesus which was destroyed by fire. Then, in the Goetheanum flames that speak to us so painfully, we shall find a reminder of what streamed out into the Akashic Record from the scorching flames of the Ephesus Temple."[36]

At the conclusion of this lecture Rudolf Steiner summarized these few sentences in the following four lines:

> "Behold the Logos
> In the scorching fire;
> Find the solution
> In Diana's house."

When the memory of Ephesus was awakened in the souls of Aristotle and Alexander at Samothrace, Aristotle was inspired to "found the cosmic alphabet". This cosmic alphabet consisted of the Aristotelian Categories: Being — Quantity — Quality — Relation — Space — Time — Position — Having — Activity — Passivity "which Aristotle first showed to Alexander". What these Categories really mean to someone who understands their origin is expressed by Rudolf Steiner in the seemingly simple words: "For all the secrets of the physical and spiritual world are contained in these simple concepts which are the cosmic alphabet."[37]

In a few sentences Rudolf Steiner then described the connection between what had occurred at that time when Aristotle at Samothrace was inspired out of the cosmic ether, and what was now taking place at the Easter conference in Dornach. "The time will come when man will find again what is truly resting as in a grave, namely the cosmic wisdom and the cosmic light. Man will learn to read once more in the great universe. He will experience the resurrection of what lay hidden in the intervening time of human evolution between the two spiritual epochs. And we, my dear friends, are here to make manifest once more the things that are hidden . . . And as on other occasions we could say: 'Anthroposophy is a Christmas experience' — so we may say today: 'Anthroposophy itself, in all its working, is an Easter experience, an experience of resurrection linked with the experience of the grave.'"[37]

This was Rudolf Steiner's way of preparing the members so that they would properly understand what was to follow. For now as the spiritual culmination of the lecture came a comprehensive revelation of what lay behind the burning of the Goetheanum and the Christmas Conference. And this was not all. As Rudolf Steiner stood there before them, the unmistakable karmic continuity between Aristotle and Rudolf Steiner himself was unveiled. Aristotle who at Samothrace in the inner emotion brought about by the mystery remembrance of Ephesus had received the inspiration for the cosmic alphabet out of the etheric cosmos; and Rudolf Steiner who in his spiritual vision and research had received the impulse for the Christmas Conference out of the Goetheanum fire. How was this impulse expressed? In a wide-ranging historical survey of the course of the ancient Mysteries, beginning with Gilgamesh and Eabani in Uruk and leading via Ephesus and Greece right up to the Anthroposophical Movement. It is a single "evolutionary memory" in which "mankind today should be able to read in the astral light about their former cultural epochs, just as an individual in later life can read in his ordinary memory about his youth. So that people might become aware of this I gave the lectures here over Christmas in such a way as to show you that it is indeed actually a matter of gathering the secrets we need today out of the astral light."[39]

Towards the end of his Easter conference lecture (22.4.1924) he expressed the connection between the two Mystery Centres, Ephesus and Dornach, in the following way:

"Even as Aristotle and Alexander used the fire of Ephesus when it flamed forth anew in their hearts, when it flamed forth in the cosmic ether and bore down to them anew the secrets that were afterwards gathered up into the very simple concepts — then even as they could use the fire of Ephesus, so will it be our part to use what has also been carried out into the ether . . . in the flames of the Goetheanum; namely all that has been intended and that shall be intended with Anthroposophy.

"But what does this imply? At the annual festival of mourning, at the time of Christmas and New Year, the very time in which our misfortune came upon us, it was granted us to send forth a new impulse *from the Goetheanum*. Why was it so? Because we may rightly feel that what hitherto was more or less an earthly thing, what was achieved and won and founded as an earthly thing, was carried forth with the flames into the cosmic spaces. Just because this misfortune came upon us, when we recognize and know the consequence of it, we may justly say: henceforth we understand that we can no longer merely represent an earthly concern, but we represent a concern of the wide etherial universe wherein the spirit lives. For the concern of the Goetheanum is indeed a concern of the far and wide ether in which dwells the spirit-filled wisdom of the world. It has been carried forth and we may now fill ourselves with the *Goetheanum impulses* coming in towards us from the cosmos.

"Take this as we will, take it as a picture. The picture signifies the deepest truth and this deep truth is expressed in simple words when we say: Since the impulse of the Christmas Conference, anthroposophical work shall be permeated with an esoteric stream. This esoteric stream is here because what was once earthly rayed forth into the cosmic spaces through the astral light that played its part in the physical fire, and because this returns again as a living power into the impulses of the Anthroposophical Movement if only we are able to receive them."[37]

All these quotations must be seen together with what Rudolf Steiner said about the Goetheanum during the Christmas Conference itself. All the things he said during the Christmas Conference taken together with the even broader statements he made three months later at the Easter conference coalesce to form a karmic envelope, a kind of condensed astral light shining around the Goetheanum. They lead not only to an extraordinary deepening of our understanding of the

Christmas Conference but also to a highly significant widening of our grasp of everything he said in connection with Aristotle in relation to his own work as leader of the Anthroposophical Movement and the Anthroposophical Society. From this point of view we may place particular emphasis on what he said on 18 July 1924 in Arnhem: "And so — let me put it this way — in the Anthroposophical Society we have Aristotelianism working on, but in a spiritualized form, and awaiting its further spiritualization."[39A]

Spiritual Events Around the Year 869

It is necessary to concern ourselves thoroughly with the lectures on karma which Rudolf Steiner gave in London, especially that of 27 August 1924.[32] This will help us to see the events, which we increasingly discover to be grouped round the Christmas Conference and the Goetheanum as the spiritual history of mankind, for what they really are: secrets we need today to be gathered out of the astral light.

This lecture is concerned particularly with the personality who reincarnated on 22 January 1561 as Francis Bacon of Verulam having lived in the 9th century as Harun al-Rashid. These connections are discussed in detail as part of the spiritual stream of the west in so far as they are relevant to the year 869 AD and the Eighth Ecumenical Council held in Constantinople.

The manner in which this is done in the London lecture and the almost tangibly concrete manner in which Rudolf Steiner described the many levels of events which took place in the year 869 give us the impression that at the place where Bacon was born and lived there must have been an unusual concentration of spiritual messages and an intensive raying out of spiritual knowledge.

The lecture describes the spiritual battle that took place at the Council of Constantinople in 869 at which the church fathers, after lengthy deliberations, established the dogma which stated that the human being was not a trichotomy consisting of body, soul and spirit but a dichotomy, consisting of body and soul, the soul having, it was conceded, some spiritual characteristics. This was a reversal of previous insight which saw man as living in three regions of existence, namely bodily, soul and spirit existence. Now only the dichotomy of body and soul held validity. This became the dogma of the catholic church and every other view of the human being was a transgression against the *true teaching*.

This dogma severed the proper knowledge of man that ought to arise as a genuine image of his creation. A proper relationship to the supersensible world that can only arise out of a view of the spiritual being of man was thus paralysed for a long stretch of time. Rudolf Steiner called the events leading to the establishment of this dogma "a specific impulse of darkness". From now on this impulse flowed into the age of the Kali Yuga, leading increasingly to a rigid, materialistic concept of man.

Now at the same time, round about the year 869, a "heavenly council" was taking place in the spiritual world itself. It came about as the result of a meeting between Harun al-Rashid and his counsellor with the individualities of Aristotle and Alexander the Great, a meeting that arose out of Harun's reverent longing for Aristotle while he had enthusiastically studied his works translated into Arabic. Now they met in the spiritual world and straight away their encounter became an intense spiritual battle between Mohammedanism, which was lodged in the soul of Harun with all the force of his aristotelian schooling, and Christianity, which had been deeply absorbed and experienced by the soul of Aristotle. Both Aristotle and Alexander had received the experience of Christianity chiefly from a *single* source: When the two friends were dwelling in the sun in the spiritual world they experienced the departure of the Christ Being from the sun on his way to the earth. In Torquay Rudolf Steiner spoke about this on 14 August 1924:

"Michael and his own, among them Alexander and Aristotle, did not experience the Mystery of Golgotha from the vantage-point of the earth; they did not witness the arrival of Christ on the earth, they witnessed his departure from the sun. And all that they experienced formed itself into the impulse which remained alive in them — the impulse to ensure that the new Michael Rulership, to which with every fibre of their souls Alexander and Aristotle had pledged their troth, would bring a Christianity not only firmly established but deeply inward, more profound."[32]

But a more hidden source of their experience of Christianity was a short incarnation in the 8th/9th century which brought them into contact with the Grail stream of esoteric Christianity.

In the spiritual Council between the souls of Harun al-Rashid and his counsellor and the souls of those two friends, Alexander and Aristotle, so newly established in Christianity and the Rulership of Michael, an understanding was not possible. Harun al-Rashid distinctly rejected an Aristotelianism permeated by Christ and linked so energetically with Michael. Two streams grew out of this confrontation: one "which took its course in Arabism, and one whereby, through the impulses of the Michael Rulership, Aristotelianism was to be led over into Christianity."[32]

The consequence of this spiritual encounter in the year 869 appeared with terrible vehemence in Bacon, the reincarnated Harun al-Rashid, as a total rejection of everything that might be considered aristotelian. For he had to discover in the 16th century that meanwhile Aristotle and Alexander had lived and worked further in the Scholasticism of the Middle Ages for a new, entirely Christianised Aristotelianism. Bacon could only cope with this discovery in his own mohammedan, arabic way. Two sentences express this in a nutshell: "Lord Bacon is a violent opponent of Aristotelianism. His passionate antagonism is so clearly in evidence that one can perceive how deeply this impulse is rooted in his soul."[32]

These two events of the year 869, the earthly and the heavenly council, are illumined by the lofty spiritual light of a third event, "the meeting of the Christ with His own image". This image is His own *Life-Spirit* which since His death on Golgotha has been working all round the globe so that "the earth is as though swathed by the element of the spirit".[32] The Christ left His *Spirit-Man* behind on the sun, His *Life-Spirit* in the surroundings of the earth, and His *Ego and Spirit-Self* on the earth.

So now in the year 869 that part of the Christ Being which had remained on the earth since the Mystery of Golgotha encountered his lofty Life-Spirit, His own image. "This flowing together of the Christ with His own image took place in the 9th century".[32]

The 9th century, which had never been particularly noted before, was shown by the many lectures of Rudolf Steiner to merit a high degree of historical awareness as a focal point of mankind's evolution. The significance of the events of 869 both on earth and in the heavens could only be revealed by Rudolf Steiner's research. It became apparent that neither past nor future could be understood without a revelation of the secret of the year 869.

The very fact that we can speak of a "secret of the year 869" shows that a profounder historical understanding is needed, for the historian is seldom confronted with historical events meriting the description "secrets". But here the hidden spiritual motifs that underlie external happenings are partly unveiled. What is the motif behind the abolition of the spirit? Why is the trichotomy of the human being rejected? What principle gained the upper hand when the threefold membering of man in body-soul-spirit was replaced by the duality of body-soul? Anthroposophical research into historical matters will always take into account that two causes have to be investigated. The one is the fact that earthly events are images of spiritual processes; the other that history runs its course in rhythms which take effect over long periods of time.

Why did the Council of 869 come about in the first place? We shall have to look as far back as the Turning Point Of Time to discover the root cause of historical sequences that reach right up to the present day and manifest as measures to prevent the spiritual progress of mankind.

In March 1917 in Berlin, Rudolf Steiner gave a cycle of lectures entitled *Building Stones for an Understanding of the Mystery of Golgotha.*[41] The very first of these (27.3.1917) gave a comprehensive and hitherto unique description of the history of the Mysteries and their spiritual background starting in Palestine and proceeding right up to the present and on into the future. The synopsis for this lecture reads: "The Palestinian Mysteries. The Pauline man: the psychic and pneumatic human being." One of the final sentences culminates in a call for a proper study of history: "When we study the real history of Europe from the rise of Christianity onwards, we are no longer satisfied with that 'fable convenue' which passes for history and which is the hidden cause of so much trouble today. And when we have sufficient courage to reject this parody of history, we shall develop a feeling which will serve as a guiding principle in our enquiries into the evolution of Christianity today. We shall discover that nothing has met with so many hindrances, so much incomprehension and misrepresentation as the evolution of Christianity."[41]

This part of the lecture is preceded by one of the unforgettable treasures of spiritual history: an introduction to the forces that are in opposition to the Mystery of Golgotha. The insight this gives into the whole interweaving complex of the Mysteries is a necessary preparation for the lectures Rudolf Steiner gave seven years later on the karma of the Anthroposophical Movement.

The matter under consideration is the constellation in which the event of Golgotha was embedded. Even the Old Testament gives an answer to this question, though the description to be found there can only be fully understood "by one who can still or once again master certain things that are connected with Imaginative cognition."[41] Emil Bock in his books on the Old Testament[42] is supremely skilled in showing us these Imaginations and throwing light on the spiritual reality of these stories. Every page contains revelations of profoundest Mystery wisdom, initiations, the deeds of initiates, guidance by spiritual beings who revealed themselves to certain human beings — a living stream of Mystery workings flowing through the land of Palestine like a spiritual Jordan, experienced and understood by very many Jews.

We become familiar with Judean history at the height of its Mystery activity. But at the same time we face like a terrible law the fact that every Mystery, even the highest, is attacked on all sides by forces of opposition. The highest initiate must learn to look into the abyss of annihilation as part of his initiation. Just as life in paradise, through the temptations of the serpent, turned into "selfhood-guilt through others incurred" and led to the earthly life of the human being, just as Moses, through his doubt as to the existence of a spiritual world, was forbidden to enter the promised land, just as Christ was accompanied by His twelve disciples, one of whom was a traitor, so was the whole work of Christ surrounded by the sect of the Sadducees who sought to fan the flames of hatred among all Jews against the Christ

Event. In the Sadducees lived the impulse to destroy everything that arose out of the Mystery cult, so they accepted neither the resurrection nor the ancient Jewish belief in angels. They shuddered with "a horror and dread of any kind of Mystery cult". And they were in control of the law courts and the administration of Palestine and were thus able to exert the pressure which led to the condemnation of Christ-Jesus. In one sentence Rudolf Steiner characterized their relationship with the Romans who ruled the country: "In effect they were the servile agents of Rome." As a result there were unusual interactions between their forces of hate and the innate Roman tendency "to forbid the harbouring of anything spiritual". The relevant passage in the lecture already quoted follows:

"It was they who realized that Rome was threatened if it should come to be accepted in any way that the drama of Christ was related to the fundamental teachings of the Mysteries. They had an instinctive feeling that Christianity would give birth to something that would gradually overthrow the authority of Rome. And this accounts for those fierce wars of extermination which Rome waged against Judaism in Palestine during the first century and in later centuries. These wars of extermination were pursued with the avowed object of exterminating not only the Jews but all those who knew anything of the reality and traditions of the ancient Mysteries. Everything associated in any way with the Mystery teachings, especially in Palestine, was to be destroyed root and branch . . . The policy of Romanism was to establish a social order in which the spirit had no place, to encourage an evolutionary trend that would exclude all spiritual impulses."[41]

In this lecture Rudolf Steiner makes us aware of extraordinarily significant aspects of the workings of the ahrimanic impulses in history. For centuries this stream sought to annul the working of the Christ Impulse with grim determination by means of war and murder which were to destroy mankind on earth. If by nothing else, the intervention of high spiritual powers in earthly evolution is made apparent simply by the reaction of the opposing forces in the way they have let loose immeasureable powers of destruction in order to make it impossible for the spirit to work. As its darker aspects show, the 20th century is no exception to this.

The battle against the spirit, as it has been grimly, cunningly and tenaciously fought during the post-Christian centuries, gained its particular stamp from the union of the spirit of Roman imperialism with the being of the Catholic church. This "marriage" became a force that was prepared to use any means in the battle against every form of Mystery working and thus also against the highest Mystery of all, the Mystery of Golgotha, so that mankind might be prevented from recognizing it for what it was.

External annihilation was not enough; inner, spiritual annihilation had to follow. This was achieved by the Ecumenical Council at Constantinople in the year 869 which took that most *successful* step of abolishing the spirit. What followed was natural science, university learning, the spread of materialism culminating in *Ignorabimus:* we shall never know! Dostoyevsky must have understood the essential nature of this ecclesiastical power when he wrote his tale of the *Grand Inquisitor.* If we follow the course of history we come to understand the burning of the Templars, the burning of the Maid of Orleans, of Giordano Bruno and countless others as attempts to banish from their incarnations those who recognized the spirit and bore the spirit of knowledge within themselves.

The attempt to view man as a dichotomy of body and soul reveals the loss of true understanding. It is impossible to build a proper life anchored in reality on such a view because the knowledge on which it is based is defective. Human life becomes confused, dependent on environment and physical heredity; it is found to be without meaning. A spiritual paralysis leading to skepticism dominates cultural life; the stranglehold of views such as Marxism is the inevitable result. Human beings come to feel their incarnation as a banishment from the spiritual world.

We cannot help but ask the disquieting question: Could not Christianity itself have overcome these powers of opposition? An answer is given by Rudolf Steiner in a statement of historical fact: "We shall discover that nothing has met with so many hindrances, so much incomprehension and misrepresentation as the evolution of Christianity. And nothing has been so difficult as its propagation. When one speaks of miracles, there is no greater miracle than this, namely that Christianity has survived, that it is still here."[41]

In order to be effective on earth, every spiritual stream needs human beings who will take it into their souls. In the prologue to the Gospel of John we read:

For the true Light which lighteth every man
  should come into the World.
It was in the World and the World came into being
  through it, but the world knew it not.
It entered into individual men (ego men);
  but individual men (ego men) received it not.

As perception of the spirit died out and the links with the spiritual world were lost, human souls turned more and more to earthly sensual existence, devoting themselves entirely to it. And as life belonged to this world alone it led men to take hold of their own personality; they became Egos. Roman culture in particular intensively cultivated the formation of the earthly personality, bound within the body and splendidly underpinned by legal rights. But the more human beings bound themselves to external existence, the more their inner soul forces diminished. The weakness of the individuality manifesting from within was shown up in the inability to comprehend higher spiritual matters. The very kernel and essence of Christianity, the Mystery of Golgotha, was no longer understood. This, too, is expressed in the Gospel of John:

But they who received it could reveal themselves
as Children of God.
They who trusted in His name were not born of the blood,
nor of the will of the flesh, nor of the will of man —
But according to the laws of the Divine Spirit.

Right up to our present day the most important aspect of an incarnation is whether the person in question can find a relationship to the Christ. When this happens the inner fountain of strength is renewed, activating the spiritual nature of man. Many souls who are today so dissatisfied and empty, so full of doubts about the supersensible world have brought this attitude with them from their former incarnation, for even then they found no opportunity to place themselves into a positive relationship with Christianity.

This shows how very possible it is for the individual human being to fall away from the spiritual stream which previously maintained his links with the Christ Event; the consequence is total aloofness from anything spiritual. This aversion and aloofness must, however, be deeply rooted in a person's particular nature. With a clarity that can shock us, the varying ways of understanding the spirit are expressed in the encounter that took place in 869 between the individualities of Aristotle and Alexander on the one hand and those of Harun al-Rashid and his wise counsellor on the other. There seem to be some souls who are so hardened towards the new spiritual impulses that there might as well be a whole universe between them.

We must set ourselves to understand these differences in people's attitudes arising out of their spiritual nature. How is it possible for any individuality to deny the spirit as vehemently as Harun al-Rashid did? The reason is given in the lecture Rudolf Steiner gave on karma on 8 August 1924.[43] To understand it we have to see and understand how earthly history arises from decisions made in the spiritual world by spiritual beings. We must now turn our attention to just such an event among higher beings which has placed a heavy burden on the history of mankind.

The year 869 is increasingly becoming a focal point, a cross-roads for the future of mankind that is to arise out of those very varied events that took place at that time. On the one hand the resolution of the Council at Constantinople to declare that man was a being of body and soul without any independent spirit nature led to consequences for earthly history. Through all the centuries since that time human cultural life has been burdened by this decree. On the other hand the union between the Christ Being and His own image, His Life-Spirit, marked the beginning of a still incomprehensible crescendo or intensification of the Christ Impulse. With our present-day consciousness we have probably still not taken in fully what Rudolf Steiner meant by this, nor have we understood its significance as a sequel to the Mystery of Golgotha. Rudolf Steiner gave no further clarification. But we shall have to become increasingly aware that this is something that calls for thorough spiritual investigation.

In the first place we shall have to take into account that Rudolf Steiner explained the decision of the Council as having to do with the actions of certain angeloi. (8.8.1924) "When the church fathers were deliberating in the year 869 whether spirit should henceforth be a matter for discussion, this was a consequence of the fact that a number of angeloi were separating from the realm of Michael where they had been before, and were assuming that they would henceforth use only earthly powers in the guidance of human beings. You must see clearly what kind of event that was! Angeloi are the beings who guide men from earthly life to earthly life . . . and now a number of angel beings — beings who have this task and who have been united formerly with the Michael kingdom — went out and left the kingdom of Michael."[43]

This event led to a division among the angel beings: one group remained with Michael while others turned towards the earth. Having been celestial angels, they now became terrestrial angels who united themselves with the earth and its earthly forces. They took up a new position in the order of the hierarchies; they left their former orderly position in the cosmos. They became angels who worked in a different way. This incisive revolution among supersensible beings of the rank of angeloi led on the one hand to the decision of the church fathers to surrender the image of man to the *earthly powers,* the ahrimanic regents so that it deteriorated into a fragmented and therefore darkened image. And on the other hand a new and infinitely tragic problem arose that has to do with karma because the angeloi are directly involved. Rudolf Steiner's own description gives the full gravity of the situation.

"But these beings themselves partake in the formation of karmic evolution. Consider the whole of this as it takes place in the life between death and a new birth. Here it is not so that every human soul can run his course alone, nor can every angel who guides the human being run his course alone; the hierarchy of angeloi work together. And in their working together karma lives and is worked out. If in an earthly life I become connected with another human being and we work this out karmically in our next life, then, needless to say, the angel of the one human being must come together with the angel of the other. A co-operation must take place, and in many cases this is just what happened. Herein lies the shattering, indeed crushing tragedy that took place on earth in the Ecumenical Council of 869. It was the signal for an overwhelming event in the spiritual world above. This event of crushing, shattering significance which started at that time and grew ever more menacing was the following: The angel of one human being, of one human soul, who was karmically connected with another human soul, did not go on with the angel of that other soul. Of two human souls karmically united with one another, the one angel remained with Michael while the other went down to earth. What was bound to happen as a result? In the time between the founding of Christianity and the age of the consciousness soul which is signalized above all by the 9th century and the year 869, the karma of human beings came into disorder! This is one of the most significant statements that can possibly be made about the more recent history of mankind."[43]

In order to understand fully the dimensions of the events that took place in the various spheres in the year 869, we must be especially aware of one fact in particular. This is that the Christ Being, Who had accomplished the Mystery of Golgotha with His Spirit-Self and His Ego, was united with His Life-Spirit, His own image "borne towards him", in the year 869 after the Turning Point Of Time, that is 836 years after the Mystery of Golgotha. Only then did this entirely cosmic being known by the name of "Life-Spirit" become united with the Christ.

We may take this to signify a cosmic crescendo, an intensification of the Christ Principle. What took place through the Christ was mirrored by the polarity of the other events: the falling away of the angeloi from Michael and their transformation into beings connected with earth forces; and also the darkening of the spiritual image of man through the decision of the Ecumenical Council.

Can we tell from this what the Christ actually did? Once in Lemurian times, twice in Atlantis, and then again in the year 33 on Golgotha this spirit being of the sun himself rescued mankind from ruin. In Basel on 1 June 1914[44] in the lecture entitled *The Four Sacrifices of Christ* Rudolf Steiner spoke especially about Christ's protection, deliverance and healing of mankind. And now all that had been won in the way of true humanity is once again in danger of being lost through what was done in the year 869 through hatred against the spirit. The events of darkness together with the falling away of the angeloi constitute a storming of the Mystery of Golgotha such as could only have been set in train by the grandest intelligence of the opposing powers. Yet when Rudolf Steiner describes this situation (27.8.1924) in words that are calm and composed, the weights start to shift:

"This all took place in the light raying from the other event, namely the meeting of Christ with His own Image. And the lines, the threads of the spiritual life of mankind were projected with great intensity in the spiritual world which borders directly on the physical world of earth."[32]

We could dwell on these few sentences for a long time, moulding them into an Imagination expressing the various regions of this earthly and yet supersensible drama. There we should see, as in Raphael's *Disputa,* a mighty panorama of argumentation surrounded by lowering clouds. But over all would shine the Spirit Sun of the new Christ encounter projecting far into the future a new spiritual life of mankind.

And who would be standing in the shining rays looking into the future growth of the new spiritual life? It would be he who had carried on the fierce battle over the future of the western world with Harun al-Rashid, that resolute opponent, namely the individuality who had once been Aristotle when he had a pupil Alexander. And words arise out of this Imagination: "But one thing was clear: one would have to wait till the new Michael Regency could begin on earth."

Clearly, this sentence expresses only the beginning of a thought. It is interrupted in a manner that challenges us to find its conclusion. "One thing was clear" — to *whom*? Obviously the reference must be to that spirit who feels utterly united with the coming of the new Michael Age at the end of the 19th century. And experiencing that apocalyptic spiritual vision, that spirit was faced with the decision to fight the battle to the very end with all his will and all his energy, making common cause with Michael with whom he shared a spiritual goal: the goal of opening the eyes of the human being to his true spiritual nature in such a way that a fiery life of inner knowledge would permeate his incarnation in the next Michael age. The brief words "one would have to wait" may have sounded as follows in this spirit-soul: *I must wait — but then in the west a fortress will be built for all mankind in which the spiritual warriors will be trained who will cause the Council of 869 to collapse upon itself. This Council must never be victorious. And the superabundance of Christ's working in conjunction with His etheric Life-Spirit will flow into a new Turning Point Of Time for all mankind.* In the lecture of 14 August 1924 it is said of Alexander and Aristotle: "But a new and mighty impulse whereby a special form of Christianity would be instilled into earthly civilization — it was to the inauguration of this impulse that Alexander and Aristotle dedicated themselves."[32]

The Rhythmic Sequences of the Year 869

The fundamental significance of the year 869 revealed by spiritual research is a considerable discovery for the historian and further investigation will prove rewarding.

Once the possession of an individual independent spirit had been denied to man by the Council of Constantinople, the far-reaching consequences of such a step began to appear and they continued to emerge as the centuries went by. The repercussions may be sought where spiritual life unfolds its particular mission: in the activation of knowledge, in the grasping of the truth, in the development of an independent individuality, and in the striving for contact with those higher worlds whose grand, all-embracing task is the spiritual evolution of mankind, namely in the first place the Spirits of Form and then also the Spirits of Personality.

The resolution of the Council is aimed particularly at this spiritual guidance by the hierarchies. It was intended to be in good time to create an obstacle against that development of mankind of which the background was discussed in the previous chapter.

To consider an early inhibition of the development of consciousness we have to turn our attention to the point in time when the age of the consciousness soul began, namely the year 1413. For 2,160 years mankind had followed the path towards the formation of the consciousness soul which has as its explicit goal the development of the ego whose nature was at first hidden but is now known. During this period the leaders of mankind intended to initiate incarnated souls into the Mysteries of the Ego. The forces of opposition, on the other hand, intended to hide the thought of the ego from mankind. This true thought was to be made indisputable and meaningless for the representatives of the faith, namely Christianity, and also for the newly emerging scientific disciplines. The Council of 869 had a period of 544 years in which to achieve this broad aim, from 869 till 1413, the year that marked the end of the fourth post-Atlantean cultural epoch and the beginning of the fifth. Measured against the whole duration of a cultural epoch, 2,160 years, this represents about a quarter.

An investigation of this last quarter of the Graeco-Roman epoch from the 9th to the 15th century reveals acrimonious disputes in all streams of life, such as the struggle between ecclesiastical and secular power, the collision between dogma and the independent search for knowledge, the power wielded by the much-feared Inquisition against any kind of freedom, the sharp philosophical disputes between realism and nominalism. All these may be seen against the background of a mighty impulse to prevent the rise of any independent, genuinely free spiritual life. It is as though the spirits of 869 were gathering together all the forces of its own cultural epoch, which was nearing its end, in order to put a final stop to any further development. No true image, no Imagination of the true nature of man was to be allowed to come about.

Rudolf Steiner spoke unequivocally of the fact that the whole development of the natural sciences in their view of the human being is a result of the year 869: the theory of evolution, the theory of heredity, education, psychology, to name but the most important. These are *defective* sciences because they lack true knowledge about the existence of the free human spirit.

This campaign of destruction against the human being has definite phases which are revealed by a scrutiny of the way it continued to work on during the fifth cultural epoch starting in 1413. Having considered the symptoms of the last quarter of the fourth cultural epoch, we can similarly investigate the first quarter of the fifth epoch as a mirror image of it. This quarter also covers 544 years, from 1413 to 1957. Just as the year 869 brought a final gathering of past strength, so the year 1957 can be seen to herald future efforts to distract man from the realities of our time.

The launching of *Sputnik I,* the first space capsule, on 4 October 1957 was the first act of a type of space research that will have consequences of which we can as yet have no realistic inkling. If we really think about the actions of technology since the beginning of the age of the consciousness soul, we can reach but one conclusion. Every *pioneering feat* of technology that has become part of civilization today has led to immense destruction and even radical annihilation in the realm of nature and biology. And in addition social problems have been created which call in question the cultural and social cohesion of mankind. So far *planetary space* has remained intact. But now the impulses and methods of technology are being carried into these realms as well. Here by their very nature they will act as focusses and forces of destruction.

It will be necessary to search for the spiritual concepts which belong to these technologies in order to reveal what mankind is really doing. Every unconsidered act committed without having worked out the concepts that belong to it leads to illusion, not to a science of reality. We may observe this, for instance, in the field of nuclear research.

One thing is certain: Every action carried out by human beings leads to effects and counter-effects. Today, for instance, we are in the midst of the consequences of the colonialism of the 18th and 19th centuries with its often inhuman suppression of the coloured races. Because of their tremendous spiritual and social impact these consequences have so far defied all attempts to find solutions. It is inevitable; irresponsible actions produce backlashes. In this connection between action and consequences is there perhaps a universal human problem setting us the imperative task of finding knowledge that can lead to answers? This question belongs to Mystery wisdom and points us towards the spiritual research of Rudolf Steiner.

Ever since ancient Greek times mankind has known that certain beings attach themselves to every human deed, unfolding their activity in the doer's aura of spirit and soul. We need only mention Orestes who was pursued and hunted by the furies, the beings of revenge, after he had murdered his mother. In this way every action attracts elemental beings who undergo a kind of incarnation in the action and thus play their part in the course of mankind's history. Every deed gains an inevitable position as a spiritually motive force that becomes a source of "counter-effects" on man and humanity. An archetypal law of karma is expressed in this: The effects always find their way back to the one who provided the cause in the first place. In a lecture given on 6 December 1919 Rudolf Steiner described the rhythms involved, speaking first of the conditions of soul in the different periods of a person's life and going on to depict how these return in accordance with the laws of the seven-year rhythm.

"The human being continously creates around himself something like a large aura. Elemental beings mix with the waves he produces, and depending on the kind of person he is, they influence the waves on their return. Imagine you are excited; this excitement rays out from you. But when it returns to you it is not as it was before because elemental beings have meanwhile been active with it. So when it then returns to you and works on you it brings with it what the elemental beings have done to it while it was outside you. Through the spiritual atmosphere he emanates, the human being enters into an interrelationship with elemental beings. Everything to do with destiny that takes place during a person's life is connected with these things. Even within one life we undergo a kind of fulfilment of our destiny."[45]

These are processes that take place not in the life of thinking and concepts but in the world of feeling and of willing. In the latter two we live subconsciously in the spiritual sphere of the elemental beings; we are integrated into this sphere which is "for us also permeated by the Christ Impulse. In physiological terms we plunge through our rhythmic system, through our feeling sphere into that region with which Christ has united Himself for earthly life. Here we find the place in which the Christ is real and can be found objectively, not only by tradition or subjective mysticism. But at the same time we are living in a period which marks the beginning of a time when the events emanating from this place . . . possess an immense objective significance for the life of man. For gradually they will gain unconscious influence over human decisions, over what people do, if they resist them. But if people work with them they can experience a conscious influence, that is they can reckon with them; we can to some extent call upon the spiritual worlds which belong to us to work with us."'[45]

It is now relevant to ask whether we can indeed experience how "the spiritual worlds which belong to us" have been called upon "to work with us". The answer to this question will show us the actual dimensions of the whole matter of how our deeds return to us eventually.

When Rudolf Steiner opened the Christmas Conference he called upon the members to activate the forces of mood and atmosphere with which they were to warm and carry the Conference. He was anxious that the waves and vibrations of the heart should be active, not the ideas and concepts of the head. Not only an individual but a whole community of like-minded people is capable of taking what is received and carried by the strong forces of feeling and fashioning from it that aura into which the elemental beings will enter, just as individually we unconsciously experience the spiritual sphere of the elemental beings. What takes place supersensibly in this way is of untold importance because this is also the region that is "woven through with the Christ Impulse". Considering the Christmas Conference in this light we realize immediately how very much this event might be experienced as taking place in the spiritual grounds of world history. And now we can grasp the immeasurable significance of those lines which appear so simply in the Foundation Meditation as a call to the elemental beings:

"The elemental Spirits hear it
In East, West, North, South:
May human beings hear it."

Rudolf Steiner issued this call to the elemental beings only once, on the opening day of the Conference, 25 December. We take it that he called only once because they had heard the call and had come to take part. But then they were called once more, when the sixth daily rhythm was given by Rudolf Steiner. And now in the meditative sequence of the lines we find an astonishing intensification, because Rudolf Steiner united the elemental spirits with the Christ Being. He introduced the meditation for this sixth day with the following words:

"Now let us impress on ourselves the words:

Light-Divine,
Christos-Sun,

in such a way that the final words, which shall be spoken in a threefold way again tomorrow are related to the manner in which this Divine-Light, this Christos-Sun shine so that they can be heard from East, West, North, South like shining suns.

"We particularly relate to this Divine-Light, to this Christos-Sun the final words we spoke on the first day:

Light-Divine,
Christos-Sun,
The elemental Spirits hear it
In East, West, North, South:
May human beings hear it!"

Thus we are accorded a glimpse into the mystery of those sub-conscious soul regions in which the elemental beings, called together by the feeling forces of human beings, collaborate with the true Christ Impulse of our time in such a way that they contribute to the task set us by our destiny.

Now in discovering something about how our deeds reverberate back on us, we have also thrown light on the laws of rhythm that work in history. With this in mind let us now immerse ourselves in the second part of the Foundation Meditation:

"Soul of Man!
Thou livest in the beat of heart and lungs,
Which guide thee through the rhythm of the Ages
Into the feeling of thine own soul-being:
Practise Spirit-Meditation
In the soul's equilibrium,
Where the surging deeds
Of Cosmic Evolution
Unite
Thine own I
With the Cosmic I;
And thou wilt truly feel
In Human Soul-Activity.
For the Christ-Will reigns in the Circumference
In the rhythms of the world blessing the souls."

Through a kind of initiation into the Deeds of Cosmic Evolution vouchsafed us here we come again to the realm of feeling in our soul-being which has the task of achieving soul equilibrium by its own inner efforts. There the Deeds of Cosmic Evolution lead our own I to unity with the Cosmic I. Within the human being himself there is a weaving together with the highest Ego Being. This takes its course in the deepest hidden grounds of the soul. It is necessary for the consciousness soul to be absolutely clear about the fact that as an actively working spiritual being it has become a factor in world history. In it the rhythms of history are worked out. It stands with a sure inner orientation in the waves of cosmic evolution because it has practised Spirit-Meditation. This is revealed to our ego if only we can grasp how the year 1957, working in the first quarter of the new cultural epoch, has taken up an impulse from the year 869 which leads on again into the future. The vital question always is whether the culture and civilization spreading over the face of the earth will allow the human ego to incarnate.

Seeing how the soul forces are bound to the body in childhood, how childhood fantasy which promotes soul activity in Imaginative capacity is paralysed by film and television, how today's incredibly abstract teaching desolates the higher artistic soul qualities, we do not find much that could be called a ruling impulse for incarnation. Even the human body from childhood on is subjected to treatment and influences of civilization which prevent it more and more from taking part in the deep life processes in connection with the development of soul and spirit. We must see that the bodily processes are becoming hardened and sclerotic. Bodies are growing up which grow old too quickly and too soon. They are no longer capable of letting soul and spirit work within them as bearers of destiny. The process of history appears to our inner vision like a succession of impulses of darkness most strongly negating the nature of the human being. In 869 the spirit is abolished, and then leading right up to the 20th century the soul is paralysed and this in turn is accompanied by a hardening of the body:[46]

869-1413-1957

Rudolf Steiner speaks quite definitely about the *abolition of the soul:* "Just as the Council of Constantinople abolished the spirit by issuing the dogma that the human being consists of body and soul, making it heretical to speak of the spirit, so in another form attempts will be made to abolish the soul and soul life. And the time will come, perhaps quite soon . . . when it will be said: Those people alone are healthy who speak only of the body. It will be seen as a symptom of illness if a person develops in a way that allows him to entertain the concept of a spirit or a soul . . . And you may be quite certain that a suitable medicine will be found . . . Out of a "healthy viewpoint" a vaccination will be developed so that the organism may be treated as early as possible, preferably at birth, to prevent the idea ever arising that there is a soul and a spirit."[47]

But this depressing picture arising out of all that followed from the deed of 869 can also act as a challenge to search for an alternative in history. We find such an alternative in the decided manner in which

Rudolf Steiner conducted research first and foremost in two scientific fields: firstly the effect on physical substances of dilution, *potentisation;* and secondly the effect that the forces of the starry constellations (Zodiac) and the planetary movements have on life processes on earth. We might also say that the courses Rudolf Steiner gave, for instance on the bio-dynamic method of agriculture in 1924, act as a therapeutic protection against the practices of materialistic planetary research that commenced in 1957. Are there causes for this, too, which may be found in the far past?

In the year 869 it was not only the Council of Constantinople that took place; there was also that other "supersensible Council". And furthermore, since then mankind's development has also been permeated by that lofty spiritual event which rays out into the etheric earth, the union of the Christ Being with His own Life-Spirit "which intensely projected the spiritual life of man". Might we not therefore hope to find not only the *earthly* but also the *spiritual* events of 869 mirrored in the year 1957?

Let us turn once more to the Christmas Conference of 1923 and focus attention on the last day (1 January 1924). The climax of the Conference was the deeply felt parting as the members bade farewell to Rudolf Steiner and to Dornach. The words Rudolf Steiner gave them to take away with them culminated in his challenge: ". . . if today in memory we resolve, each before the best and most divine within our soul, to remain true to the spiritual impulses . . ." This was the day on which a spiritual vow arose out of the deepest grounds of souls, out of heart forces deeply moved, together with a decision of the will to be unbreakably faithful. What took place in the souls of those present was united with the spiritual world, with the kingdom of the elemental beings and with the historical foundation of Christ. Here was something that would work on spiritually; a seed was sown which will ray back again, now permeated with the forces of the beings who participated in spirit. Since Golgotha the historical rhythm of 33 years has been imprinted on human evolution. Every deed undergoes a resurrection after 33 years. And so the deed of 1924 entered into the history of mankind and underwent its resurrection in the aura of 1957. Two threads run through the historical rhythms of time:

The year 869 is connected rythmically with 1413 and also with 1957. But the latter is also spiritually irradiated by the 33 year rhythm of 1924. So the rhythm pulse of 869 no longer works alone in the darkness but is illumined and permeated through by the Christ Stream of the Christmas Conference.

The *Christmas Conference* itself is enveloped by an aura of Christ quality: it is a totally free deed. It is not a link in the chain of rhythmic sequences but the source of a new and creative impulse in history. Through it Rudolf Steiner has created entirely new circumstances which enable a real Turning Point Of Time to take place. In accordance with his decision during the supersensible Council, he places his work in freedom at the service of the new Regency of Michael as time spirit. And in conjunction with Michael the source for a new therapy of mankind's evolution is hewn out of the eternal ground of the spirit and transformed into a stream of renewal. All the machinations of the spirits of darkness have since been met with these deeds which threaten them with ruin. For one of the greatest in the hierarchy of men, a leader in the spirit, has laid the foundation for a new history of mankind.

The Continued Working of the Christmas Conference

The new Regency of Michael began in 1879. Rudolf Steiner, born in 1861, began to tackle his life's task even as a young boy. Living in relative poverty with no external wealth to aid him, yet quite independently and free of tradition, filled with his own direct spiritual experiences, he prepared to lay the foundation of his spiritual knowledge courageously and forcefully out of his own spiritual source.

In an address on 11 April 1912 to Russian anthroposophists who had gathered in Helsinki to hear his lectures he said the following: "It has been the task of Central Europe to deliver Theosophy from the special idiosyncrasies with which it had become adorned in Western Europe. It was our mission to extricate Theosophy from all special interests. The more you go into these matters the more you will find that I myself have been able to free everything I have been permitted to place before you in the way of Theosophy from any special interest. Symbolically speaking I simply had to let myself be guided by something that was a direct impulse in my present incarnation. Please do not misunderstand me; this is simply a fact. The external bearers of the blood relationship into which I was born came from a German region of Austria; but I could not be born there. I was born in a Slav region which was entirely foreign to all the milieu and traditions of my ancestors. Thus, symbolically speaking, at the very start of my present incarnation I began to understand spontaneously that we in Middle Europe have the task of extricating Theosophy from all special interests, so that in middle Europe it may appear before us as something divine, utterly and entirely free of all human interests. Then it will have just as much to do with one who lives *here* as with one who lives *there*; and this must always remain so."[48]

The way in which he carried out this impulse of freedom is

characteristic of the spirit of Rudolf Steiner. He acted not in accordance with directives and maxims but out of the intuitions of the free human being.

But even the free human being must have his place within the laws of history. Even he must take into account the possibilities offered by the situation in which he finds himself. Consciously and thoughtfully he must consider how he stands with his own impulses at the present moment in history.

Some entries made in a notebook in 1924 reveal how Rudolf Steiner looked back on certain rhythms of his life. On the first page we find the following calculation:

1869 = 8
869

The thought contained in these figures might be formulated as follows: A thousand years after the Council of Constantinople, in the year 1869, I was a child of eight. My biography is linked to this thousand year cycle. Then come further figures which show his age in different years, starting with his birth in 1861:

1861	1861	1897	1861
21	28	1861	42
1882	1889	36	1903

1888 Ahriman is wrecked
1861
27

These are accompanied by the following text:

"My own 'intellectual soul' (28-35) is held from 1889 to 1896 in the etheric world directly bordering the sense world. From 1882 to 1889 (21-28) = I am entirely in the spiritual world which borders on the sense world.

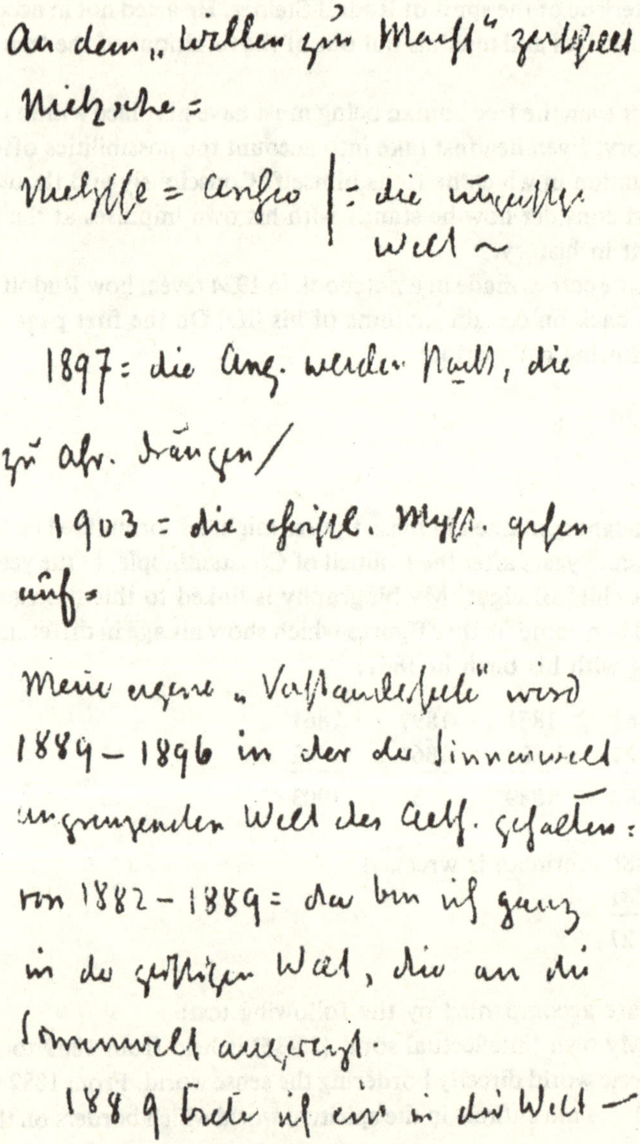

An dem „Willen zur Macht" zerschellt
Nietzsche =
Nietzsche = Ansch. | = die materielle
Welt ~

1897 = die Ang. werden Nacht, die
zur Abr. drängen /
1903 = die christl. Myst. gehen
auf.

Meine eigene „Verstandesseele" wird
1889–1896 in der der Sinneswelt
angrenzenden Welt des Geist. gehalten:
von 1882–1889 = da bin ich ganz
in der geistigen Welt, die an die
Sinneswelt angrenzt.
1889 trete ich ein in die Welt —

Facsimile from one of Rudolf Steiner's notebooks

1869 : 8

869

18

1888 zerschellt Uform

1861

27.

1897

1861

36 = 21-28

28-35

35-42.

1861

42

1903

1861

28

1889

1861

21

82

die in den Angel.-Verz. die materielles Leben angenommen hat;

es gibt da eine der menschl.-verschiedenen geist. Welt, die mat. ist; aber die das Materielle auf geistige Art offenbart/

world.

In 1889 I enter the world which, in the terrestrial angeloi, *has accepted the material teachings,* — there is also a human post-earthly similar world which is material, but this reveals the material in a spiritual way.

1897 = the angeloi pressing towards Ahriman grow strong/
1903 = the Christian Mysteries open up".

This part of the notes, too, gives us insight into the connections he saw between his own biography and the historical situation of the world at the end of the 19th century. His position in certain supersensible worlds at the beginning of the new Michael Age revealed to him the further working of those angeloi who had fallen away from the Rulership of Michael and taken on the character of terrestrial angels. The extent to which he had taken up the battle against the opponent of Michael, Ahriman, is shown in the brief calculation that concerned him particularly:

$$\begin{array}{rl} 1888 & \text{Ahriman is wrecked} \\ \underline{1861} & \\ 27 & \end{array}$$

At the age of 27, Rudolf Steiner had to give a lecture in Vienna on the theme of *Goethe as the founder of a new Science of Aesthetics.*[49] This lecture must have been a powerful spiritual experience for him. Afterwards a conversation took place in which the Cistercian priest Wilhelm Neumann "made the extraordinary statement: The seeds for the lecture you gave us today may be found in Thomas Aquinas!"[50]

Later, on 12 September 1924, Rudolf Steiner described this event with more karmic detail: "A priest of the Cistercian Order was there — a remarkable and excellent man. When I had finished my lecture, he made a very peculiar remark, the nature of which I will only indicate by saying: he uttered words in which was contained his memory of having been together with me in a former life on earth."[51]

In his biography *The Course of my Life* Rudolf Steiner wrote in the seventh chapter: "During the time I am now describing I gained through spiritual perception a definite insight into man's repeated earth-lives. Certainly, I had this insight before this time, but more in broad outlines, not in clearly defined impressions. I did not speculate about things like repeated earth lives; I accepted this as something self-evident when meeting it in literature or in any other way, but I did not theorise about it. The fact that I was conscious of a direct insight into this sphere made possible my conversation with Professor Neumann, referred to earlier."[3]

And the eighth chapter begins with the following sentences: "At this period of my life — about 1888 — I felt on the one hand impelled to strong spiritual concentration by my inner soul life . . . I was editing the second volume of Goethe's scientific writings. The detailed introduction I was to write made it necessary that I should present my views of the spirit in the form of transparent thoughts."[3]

We see from these autobiographical remarks that round about his twenty-eighth year Rudolf Steiner was engaged in strenuous inner work in exploring the spiritual world and that he was undergoing concrete experiences of repeated earth lives. Concrete experiences: he gained a view by actual experience of his relationship to Thomas Aquinas and also to Aristotle. Indications to this effect may be found in many of his lectures. To someone who is versed in Anthroposophy they reveal clearly what is meant and give a basis for understanding the lectures he gave on the one hand in *Occult History. Historical Personalities and Events in the Light of Spiritual Science*[52] and on the other as the culmination of his revelations about reincarnation, at the Christmas Conference in 1923 in the lectures *World History in the Light of Anthroposophy.*[53]

The spiritual research that Rudolf Steiner carried out throughout his life made it possible for spiritual knowledge in an extraordinary degree to become once again the focal point of human life. It became a foundation for a new spiritual life of the west. It is obvious that a deed of such magnitude would be strongly opposed by all the forces of Ahriman. The outcome of this dangerous confrontation in which

The second Goetheanum

this spiritual warrior found himself at the age of twenty-seven — amid a world of slumbering souls — could hardly be described more laconically or tersely than the notebook entry "1888 Ahriman is wrecked". This man who represents the Michael Age pursued his goal step by step, battle by battle, victory by victory. And Ahriman is wrecked.

By this full overview of his life and by the knowledge of his spiritual path over thousands of years, the final years of his incarnation are fully illuminated. The laying of the Foundation Stone in 1913, for instance, gains a new significance as a milestone in the revelation of the spiritual world and is illumined by the light of the Cosmic Prayer. And the Christmas Conference in 1923 is seen as the loftiest event of thousands of years of human history when we realize that it opened the flood-gates of the spirit and washed away what had been set up by Ahriman's powers of darkness around the year 869. "One would have to wait" it is said in the karma lectures of 1924 when Rudolf Steiner united christianized Aristotelianism with the Anthroposophical Movement to form the Michael Stream of our time, describing it in its great karmic context (14.8.1924):

"In one way or another, those who with deep sincerity feel the urge to enter the Anthroposophical Society are linked to events like the meeting of Alexander and Aristotle with Harun al-Rashid and his wise counsellor. Something of the kind has determined the karma which now, in the present earthly life, takes the form of longing to receive the spiritual knowledge that is cultivated in the Anthroposophical Movement."[32]

Thus when all these souls were gathered together at the grounds of the Goetheanum for the nine days of the Christmas Conference, all those were present who, like Alexander and Aristotle, had been teachers in the supersensible School of Michael. All those were gathered together who had taken part in the spiritual struggle with Harun al-Rashid and his circle. But not only those souls were present who had incarnated into the Anthroposophical Society out of the Michael Stream of that time. Just as Rudolf Steiner had invited the members to attend the

Foundation Meeting in Dornach, so, on a higher level, the invitation had been extended to the leading powers of the spiritual world and to such great individualities, for instance, as Christian Rosenkreutz or Novalis who were among the forerunners of Anthroposophy and bearers of the Michael impulse. We must not forget that the Foundation Verses were spoken "with the will of the spiritual world" and that "Anthroposophy is a service to the Gods". This means that the Christmas Conference must be seen as a Council with the high beings of Michael's Rulership and with all those members who had passed through the portals of death. Those present on earth, through their spiritual mood and their spiritual enthusiasm, stepped over the threshold *into this* spiritual gathering.

The Anthroposophical Society was consecrated as the vessel which would contain the Anthroposophical movement. And as a solemn service on earth to the Spirits it is necessary to raise men's consciousness in order to cultivate the work for the continued presence of the event of the Christmas Conference.

By emphasizing the continued presence of the Christmas Conference so strongly, Rudolf Steiner was expressing the spiritual fact that he as a leader in the Rulership of Michael would continue his work in this spiritual stream together with the others who belonged to it, permeated by the rays of the Christos-Sun and by the spirit known as Michael, the Countenance of Christ. This points to the unshakeable firmness of the Christmas Conference as an event belonging to the spiritual world. People, that is the members, are free either to muster the will to remain true to this *Council of Dornach* or to succumb to the opinion that the Christmas Conference did not succeed.

Because of its great spiritual significance we shall now consider in more detail the *continued working of the Christmas Conference.* Rudolf Steiner's words about this in the Stuttgart lecture of 6 February 1924 may accompany us in this consideration. On another occasion also, almost like a plea to his listeners, he gave a most serious characterization of the Christmas Conference using phrases which express a deeply hidden plea, almost impossible to put into words; which is addressed not only to the members but to mankind at large:

"A certain responsibility in the soul is involved when attention is directed to the Christmas Conference — the responsibility to make it a reality; otherwise it will withdraw from earthly existence and go the same way as the moon beings of which I have spoken today. Of course in a certain sense the impulse of the Christmas Conference was actually in the world. Whether it will become effective in life depends upon whether its impulse continues. This was expressed quite clearly. The spiritual Foundation Stone of the Anthroposophical Society was laid in the hearts of every participant. We brought the meeting to a formal conclusion, but actually this Christmas Conference should never be closed, it should continue perpetually in the life of the Anthroposophical Society . . .

"It has come about that at the age when people usually retire, I have made a beginning, for in fact I regard what happened at the Christmas Conference in Dornach as a beginning, a genuine beginning in life . . . Let us then work together, realizing the deep significance and seriousness of the Dornach Conference . . . Then it will have been much more than a festival week; it will be an impulse affecting the whole world and the destiny of man. And that is the right impulse for all anthroposophical work and activity and life."[63]

What *pleas* to human souls are contained in these words? They are:

— Work together from now on.
— Regard the Christmas Conference as something serious.
— Realize that it contains something that will affect the whole world, the whole destiny of mankind.
— Do not evade the decision which can cause the Christmas Conference to become "either all or nothing for the cause of Anthroposophy. It will be as nothing if it does not endure . . . It will be a reality through what it causes to happen, through what it continues to bring about in the life of the Anthroposophical Society."[63]

In these words Rudolf Steiner is wrestling for spiritual alertness in mature human souls. The Christmas Conference had taken place in a sphere of highest consciousness. If this *life beginning* that meant so much to him was really to become an impulse through which the whole of Anthroposophy would flow into work and life, then it needed true understanding, true commitment and continued life, that is the spirit, the hearts and the will of the members.

Even the Greatest One on earth long ago needed human souls who would create a sheath for his mission through sharing his experience. That was at the first Turning Point Of Time when the three most advanced disciples should have remained awake and conscious to take their part in bearing the Mystery through to its conclusion. Yet — they slept. At the Turning Point of the year 1923 once again a sheath was needed, woven of soul material made of inner understanding, total absorption in events and the resolve *to be present and to remain faithful and endure*. Was Rudolf Steiner left alone?

Understanding was present at first as a deeply moving though as yet inexpressible experience, less accessible to start with to full consciousness.

Total absorption in the impulse of the Christmas Conference became for many members the substance of their destiny.

The *contined endurance* of the Christmas Conference was exposed most of all to the attacks of all-embracing forces of destruction. They called in question the endurance of the Christmas Conference, for a continuation is inextricably linked to the shared life direction and the shared will direction that comes of working together. But at the same time endurance is also linked to continuity in the stream of time which inhabits spiritual life like an etheric body. We are touching here on a secret that lies hidden in the principle of the higher Life-Spirit. We may discover something of it if we turn our enquiry to the heavenly Council of 869 in order to seek there the source of spiritual endurance as a life principle. To do this let us consider once more the description Rudolf Steiner gave on 27 August 1924 in London:

"In the spiritual world which borders on our physical earth — it was here that Alexander and Aristotle met with Harun al-Rashid and his counsellor to consult together as to the further progress of Christianity in Europe, with an eye to what was to come at the end of the 19th century and in the 20th century, when Michael would again have the Rulership on earth . . . Such was the real course of events. In the physical world the Council of Constantinople which abolished the spirit, and in the world immediately bordering on the physical, a heavenly Council which took the form of the meeting of Christ himself with His Own Image."[32]

This meeting of the Christ with His Own Image is the meeting "with His Life-Spirit". For Rudolf Steiner then continues to describe this cosmic process: "The Christ Himself, the Christ Who had come down to earth leaving His *Spirit-Man* on the sun and His *Life-Spirit* in the atmosphere around the earth, bringing down His Ego and His Spirit-Self to the earth — the Christ was moving from East to West . . . towards Europe."[32]

From this union of the Christ's Ego and Spirit-Self with his Life-Spirit that worked in the environment of the earth went forth the bright rays of spirit which filled all that took place for mankind in the various regions in 869. Even that dark impulse that was to deprive man of his spirit was no exception. By this heavenly Christ Council that shone on all things the spiritual life of man was *projected* in a spiritual decision that was to take effect in the future. When we follow the sweep of historical links that leads from 869 to the present working of Michael in the 20th century bringing us right up to the Christmas Conference, we have to understand that the new union between the Christ's being of Ego and Spirit-Self working on the earth and His Life-Spirit streaming through the surroundings of the earth must be the central event of the Turning Point Of Time in 1923. The coming together of the members of the Christ Being, first mentioned to us in the karma lecture in London, is a fact which must lead us to a new understanding of the age in which we live, for this union in heaven was mirrored on earth by the coming together of the Grail stream and the Arthur stream.

If we manage to see the Christmas Conference and all the spiritual processes that are connected with it in such a way that it is removed from the normal criteria for conferences, then we should also be able to see the etheric future of mankind living in its stream.

Now we also gain quite a new understanding of Rudolf Steiner's statement that it would have been better never to have gathered together in the first place if the Christmas Conference is seen as nothing but an ordinary conference. We feel in it the lofty working of a great cycle of history which annuls all earthly yardsticks. It is the Spirit of Mankind himself who works in the event which we call the Christmas Conference.

So new light is also thrown on the question of how the Christmas Conference continued to endure after it had been formally brought to a close.

A short reply is that Rudolf Steiner himself gave the comprehensive answer through his work right up to the day of his death on 30 March 1925. In all his spiritual revelations, which then contained above all the inconceivable universe of research into karma, he brought the stream of the Michael Mystery down to earth. For "descriptions of karma are Michael secrets". From the point of view of world history he fulfilled a task of cosmic proportions by giving these Michael secrets as fundamental knowledge to the mainstream of culture. By ineradicably anchoring within the human being the spiritual nature of the individuality, Rudolf Steiner overcame the impulse of darkness of the Council of 869.

In the spiritual life of our time the Anthroposophical Movement must continue to work on from individual to individual. Let us look in this connection at what has come about as a result of the schism in the hierarchy of the angeloi.

When certain angeloi, beings who guide human destiny, severed their connections with the community of Michael, it became impossible for some people, whose destiny should have brought them together, to reach any form of community. Such far-reaching earthly and cosmic disturbances resulted that it became almost impossible for any kind of spiritual and social order to establish itself among men. Karmic relationships were as though suffocated, with the result that karmic compensation could not take place and people's inner development was blocked. Unfinished karma could no longer have led to any kind of compensation; a great mountain of burdens would have been built up under the weight of which human souls would have had to abandon their higher goals. Paralysis of the soul forces would have followed, leading to the *animalization* of the human being.

The prospect arising out of the opposition of certain angeloi against Michael is so gloomy and depressing that there seems to be no way out of this decline of human life.

Once we realize this as clearly and emphatically as possible, we shall come to comprehend the full magnitude of Rudolf Steiner's achievement in bringing into the mainstream of culture right at the beginning of the Michael age the knowledge of reincarnation and karma. Anthroposophy, as the most concentrated spiritual stream in which the leading beings of the cosmos gathered with Michael around the Christ, was founded by Rudolf Steiner to initiate the battle that is to rescue and set free the culture of mankind at the end of the present century. The Christmas Conference was both an archetypal image and a mirror image of this deed: source and origin, beginning of life, Turning Point Of Time.

The meeting of anthroposophical groups to carry on that work which enters into the hearts of men as Anthroposophy, adding permanent building stones to the *Goetheanum,* this is what brings about the continuation of that which entered the world as the Christmas Conference. Work is done to bring order into karma, so that human destiny may once more be properly controlled. But there is an aspect that must be emphasized:

Rudolf Steiner remains joined to his high spiritual work and we maintain our links with him so long as we understand what is meant when it is said that his name must never be separated from his work.

This significant statement, which can be a spiritual leitmotif, an exhortation and a basis for judgment for much that goes on in the Society, is contained in two communications that have been handed down to us.

In an essay dated 28 June 1925 Ita Wegman wrote: "We must preserve continuity in our work right down to its very form, so that no fragmentation or separation can take place between the anthroposophical body of wisdom and the personality of Rudolf Steiner. For he himself once said: Once I have departed from the physical plane, if the opposition forces then succeed in separating Anthroposophy from me by allowing the broad masses of humanity to hear of the teachings without knowing anything about me, it would become superficial, and this would be just what the ahrimanic beings want and intend."[54]

And in her essay *Welches sind die Aufgaben des Nachlassvereins?* (What are the tasks of the Nachlass-Verein?) Marie Steiner wrote: "He spoke to me about the time when he would no longer be among us, when it would fall to me to stand up for his work and strive to maintain the link between this great work for mankind and his name. He said that only a few would remain faithful to him and that if his work were to become separated from his name it would become estranged from its original intentions. Then the opposing powers would seize the forces contained in it and use them for their own purposes." (July 1945)

These words must continue to be noted in the future. They are one of the indications of the way in which members must work.

A Possible Successor

In the Statutes[55] of the *Anthroposophical Society,* Paragraph 7 is exceptionally significant because the rule it contains is of central spiritual importance within the totality of the Statutes. Yet at the Christmas Conference the members did not take the opportunity to ask questions. This is perfectly understandable, for each one of those present must have felt deeply reticent about starting a discussion on the subject or even expressing any curiosity about it.

Paragraph 7 runs as follows: "The establishment of the School of Spiritual Science is, to begin with, in the hands of Rudolf Steiner, who will appoint his collaborators and his possible successor."

This one sentence contains stipulations for three related matters:

1. The establishment of the Free High School;
2. The appointment of Rudolf Steiner's collaborators;
3. The appointment of his possible successor.

These three points are entirely the affair of Rudolf Steiner and are reserved for him alone.

It was then and it is still today obvious to every member that the only person who could make decisions about these matters was the one who, both factually and spiritually, was competent to found, establish, build up and run the High School. Paragraph 7 thus contains everything that is connected to the spiritual aspect of the leadership, a position which only Rudolf Steiner could hold. This obviously included the appointment of his colleagues who became necessary as soon as the High School started to expand its work. It applies, for instance, to the appointment of the Section Leaders who in the sense of Paragraph 7 were Rudolf Steiner's colleagues.

For a long time the same applied to the third point also: namely that the appointment of his possible successor as leader of the High School could only, quite rightly, be made by Rudolf Steiner himself. When it became apparent after his death that he had not appointed a successor — this must not be confused with the chairmanship of the Vorstand — this fact was accepted in accordance with Paragraph 7. But today it is necessary to express thoughts on this matter which may lead to a discovery in this very clear ruling of something which might allow us to ponder more deeply on the question of the possible successor.

It is worth remembering, first of all, that Rudolf Steiner was probably the only person to give any particular consideration, even before the Christmas Conference, to the question of a successor. The *Statutes of the Anthroposophical Society* were printed before the beginning of the Conference. Thus while working on the Statutes it was already clear to him that one day the question of a successor would have to be faced and that the only solution would be for him to appoint one. The obvious simplicity of the case is rendered puzzling, however, because even at that time an *eventuality* is expressed, a *possible* successor.

This was taken to denote that the matter was as yet quite unsettled, that there was a *possibility: if* a successor were to be found, then he would have to be appointed by Rudolf Steiner. If, on the other hand, no successor were to be found, then the position of the leader of the High School would have to remain unfilled. So the word *possible* described a situation that was not as yet resolved. The members were thus unequivocally given to understand that a situation might arise in which they would have to continue their work without a designated successor because such a person either did not exist or had not been found. This was sufficient clarification of every aspect of the succession.

As time went on, however, considerations started to appear which clouded the absolute certainty of the situation. Two questions in particular demanded an answer. Firstly, why had Rudolf Steiner found it necessary at all to bring up the question of the succession in the *Statutes* if it could not yet be settled clearly and unequivocally? Was it necesary to include an eventuality in the Statutes instead of leaving this question to life and coming to grips with it at the point when a direct solution could or had to be found?

Secondly, had the problem of the possible successor really been understood in all its complexity, or had those considering it perhaps become caught in a one-sided train of thought?

The one-sided train of thought may be outlined as follows: Before his approaching death, Rudolf Steiner would have had to appoint his successor. But this appointment would have depended on whether a person capable of leading the High School was to be found. If no such person could be found then the appointment could not be made and the High School would from then on be without a leader.

The almost incomprehensible situation would then have to be faced in which Rudolf Steiner would have called a Free High School into existence with the utmost seriousness, a Free High School, which, if no successor were appointed, would have no means of coping with this most difficult situation. And yet Rudolf Steiner's call to maintain the *Christmas Conference* and cultivate its spiritual stream would still have remained. In the spirit of this call the Vorstand, without a leader of the High School, would have to guide and administer the Anthroposophical Society as an esoteric Vorstand.

In this way many considerations ought to be thought through and faced. Also we ought to ask how the consecration of the Society through the spiritual Foundation Stone laid in the etheric hearts of those present in accordance with the will of the spiritual world is linked to the absence of a leader of the High School.

The spiritual wholeness of the archetypal image of the unity between Movement and Society ought never to be called into question, for the Christmas Conference was a *mystical fact*.

Next we must seriously consider a question that is beginning to emerge with some force: Did Rudolf Steiner himself think in this way? Did the consequences of not appointing a successor, with all the fundamental lack of certainty this would lead to, remain hidden from him?

The answer to this can hardly be other than No. All this cannot have lived in this way in Rudolf Steiner's spirit. Only one conclusion is possible: The problem posed right at the start by the question of a "possible" successor must be understood from a new angle!

Perhaps a new way can be found of understanding what is actually quite a depressing situation. Let us call up before our souls a number of Rudolf Steiner's actions which we have so far not considered. It is a fact, for instance, that Rudolf Steiner gave instructions and wrote essays, such as his biography, right up to the last day of his life. As late as 15 March 1925 he gave clear and precise instructions about the transfer of the leadership of the Free Waldorf School from himself to the college of teachers. On this date he also signed membership cards for the First Class.

On the other hand he did not *bid farewell* either verbally or in writing to the founding Vorstand he had formed during the Christmas Conference. He gave them neither guidelines nor good advice. He departed — without a word!

In an article for the *Mitteilungsblatt* of 26 April 1925, Ita Wegman, who attended him as his physician during his illness, wrote the following about the final hours of his life:

"In full consciousness, but without speaking a word about the future, without leaving any instructions or messages for one person or another, the Master went away from us. The answer to a direct question along these lines was a conscious No."[19]

It is not easy to understand this conduct. It is uncommon and poses a difficult riddle. Indeed we may say that without a proper understanding of it, our soul can hardly avoid being burdened by it.

What does Rudolf Steiner's silence say to us? Did he expect a different, more mature understanding? Or did he expect to be asked about all this much earlier on?

We might imagine a member, approaching him after the Christmas Conference, maybe for a personal private conversation, saying: What do you mean, Herr Doktor, when in point seven of the Statutes you speak of a *possible* successor? Why do you say *possible*? Surely there must always be a successor? The High School must have a leader — otherwise how can it continue to function?

And the answer he could have given might have been: We must remember that the *High School* is intended to be a Michael School and that it was not founded out of the human will but by the initiative of that being himself, out of the will of the spiritual world. The leadership of the High School is therefore a purely spiritual matter, it is the task of Michael, the Time Spirit. When in the lessons of the First Class instruction is given about special spiritual paths and special spiritual exercises, then the members have to learn something entirely new, something that belongs to the very nature of this Mystery Centre. They will hear the words being spoken by the mouth of Rudolf Steiner, but they will have to experience that in reality the indications stem from the spiritual world and have their source in the being of Michael. This understanding must definitely be one of the tasks of esoteric development. The appointment of a "possible successor" means that such an appointment is not an earthly, human affair but a lofty spiritual matter. Whatever Michael may decide will have to be accepted as destiny, as a trial of destiny or as a spiritual command. Therefore a clear indication had to be given, even in the Statutes. From the beginning the members had to be made aware of the fact that at the opening of the Christmas Conference it had been clearly stated that the *Foundation Stone Verses* were spoken "with the will of the spiritual world". The way in which the Christmas Conference proceeded from day to day clearly showed the guidance of the spiritual world, for this was present in everything that happened. This could be quite clearly and naturally experienced. The members will have to grow accustomed to taking the guidance of the spiritual world seriously.

The conversation outlined here might later have been followed by others. For instance Rudolf Steiner might have pointed out that although he had taken on himself the chairmanship of the Society, the spiritual world had allowed its revelations to stream towards him in even greater abundance than before. In the way he spoke we may perceive how relieved and glad he was about this. It signified *a new attitude of the spiritual world towards him* which he did not define in so many words but which he indicated by mentioning the spiritual reality of this new abundance. From the Christmas Conference onwards Rudolf Steiner was accepted and confirmed by the Leaders of human destiny and given a new spiritual dignity which raised him up and gave him powers to a degree which is beyond our imagination. He did not speak about this but it was apparent in his deeds and actions.

The statement that Rudolf Steiner's work must not be separated from his name also needs to be considered in connection with the problem of a successor. For from the Christmas Conference onwards the work — which includes the founding and formation of the Society — and the being of Rudolf Steiner became one and the same. He was present wherever his work was cultivated and taken up as spiritual life blood. He did not separate himself from his work. When someone spent a lifetime studying this work and striving for understanding and revelation, Rudolf Steiner was united with this striving and gave both revelation and understanding. And when the Society underwent immeasurable suffering along the path of its destiny, he lived and suffered in this affliction also.

On Sunday 28 September 1924 Rudolf Steiner rose once more from the sick bed that had been set up for him in the Atelier. He had had to cancel his lecture for Friday 26 September because he had been too weak to give it and had since remained in the Atelier, hoping to recover. For years it had been his custom to give a lecture to the members on Sunday evenings, and when the time came he forced himself with all his will power to give the Michael lecture[64] in which he wanted to present a particular result of his research. He had investigated more deeply the connection between John the Baptist and Lazarus. The solemn culmination was the Michael Meditation. But he was unable to conclude the lecture and broke off before he had finished. As he left the platform all the members rose to their feet and in this moving silence filled with veneration and love for him he dragged his weak body back to the Atelier.

There he lay, physically too weak to carry on his former activities but spiritually continuing without rest to write his biography, the medical book and the "Leading Thoughts for the Members" which reflected the light of the spiritual sun like jewels.

He never gave up hoping that his health would be restored. But he was not faced solely with the weakness of his bodily forces. He knew that the opponents of his spiritual work were capable of employing certain occult influences which could destroy him physically. A poem in his notebook for November 1924 bears witness to this. The following version was published in *Wahrspruchworte*:[21]

"Du Widersinnszauber des Lebens,
Du scheinest in der Nacht,
Und hehren Schicksalswebens
Gottgewollte ew'ge Macht
Durchlöchert die Gegenkraft —
Dass seelenquälend sich verbreitet,
Was dämonisch Unheil schafft
Und nach Schlangenart an mich gleitet."

("In the night there shines the sorcery that makes a mockery of life; the divinely-willed eternal might of destiny's sublime weaving is pierced by the opposition forces. So torturing the soul there now expands what kindles devilish calamity and slithers serpentwise towards me.")

The forces of destruction had been summoned against everything that took place in Dornach ever since the Goetheanum had been built. Rudolf Steiner had made many remarks pointing to the working of these forces, for instance: "This is connected with the fact that very powerful demonic forces are attacking the Anthroposophical Movement." He was able to resist all these onslaughts until, after the burning of the Goetheanum, the situation changed as a result of his physical weakness.

After his death these onslaughts against the Society multiplied immeasurably, bringing about virtually insoluble problems. That Rudolf Steiner continues to work can be seen in the fact that the Society persevered and the members found one another again. A kind of spiritual renewal in the initiatives also shows this.

The continued working of Rudolf Steiner provides the answer to the following question: When he closed his eyes and departed from his body on 30 March 1925, why did he not *take leave* of anybody? The answering question is: If you are not going away, why should you take your leave? Why is it stated in the printed Statutes that it was for Rudolf Steiner to appoint his *possible* successor? Has the word *possible* been mistakenly interpreted? Can it only be taken to mean that he did not appoint a successor because no such person existed? Maybe this *is* what it means. But it could equally well signify that there was no need to appoint a successor because he had taken the leadership of the High School into his own care and had not relinquished it since he had not gone away. At the time when the Statutes were printed, this high dispensation to stay was as yet entirely undecided, so at the moment it was still necessary to speak of a *possible* successor.

Rudolf Steiner's statement that his name must not be separated from his work would then quite concretely apply also to the leadership of the High School which he had been unable to pass on to a successor. In all confidence we may say that it is a spiritual reality:

Rudolf Steiner did not, by his death, separate himself from the High School, the Michael School which is a purely spiritual institution. If he remained connected with anything at all, then it was with the leadership of the High School!

In the third Mystery Drama "The Guardian of the Threshold" Benedictus expresses in the sixth scene a law that binds the spiritual teacher:

"I must bear company with everyone who has received
the spirit light from me on earth,
if he with knowledge, or unconsciously
has come to me as student of the spirit.
And I must guide him further on the paths
on which he has set out through me."

The question of Rudolf Steiner's *successor* is ever and again linked to the fact of his death. This means we must consider whether the death of such a high initiate can be compared with that of an ordinary mortal. Since he was constantly crossing the threshold in the course of his spiritual research, should not his final crossing be measured with quite another yardstick and be seen to involve quite other processes? This question is so unusual that we shall have to seek the answer in a lecture Rudolf Steiner gave in 1904 on *The Philosopher's Stone.* Here we may find a statement that leads us far beyond our present ordinary knowledge:

"The Philosopher's Stone serves a certain purpose . . . And we are not concerned here with physical death but with the following: For one who has come to understand the Philosopher's Stone . . . physical death is only a semblance. For other people it is a real event signifying a tremendous step in life. But for one who, as Cagliostro attempted with his pupils, has done this work on himself and has achieved its purpose, death is only a seeming event. It does not even signify a particularly important step into a new phase. It is real enough for those who are maybe able to observe the adept. They say that he dies. But he himself does not die at all in reality. He has learnt to cause all the processes to take place in his physical body which actually do take place in the physical body at the moment of death. Gradually throughout his life, one by one, he causes the processes to take place which occur in the physical body at the moment of death. Everything that normally occurs at death has already taken place in the body of the adept. So now death is no longer possible. He has learnt in advance how to live without a physical body which he now takes off as though it were a raincoat . . . This is the Philosopher's Stone which reduces death to insignificance."[56]

It is understandable that a particular objection is raised to the above interpretation of certain riddles of the latter part of Rudolf Steiner's life. It is objected that the interpretation of Rudolf Steiner's death as something out of the ordinary is something from the realms of mysticism. We ought to remember that we are living on the physical earth which has laws of its own that are immutable. If somebody has passed through the gate of death, which Rudolf Steiner indubitably did, then he cannot still be the leader of the High School in the same way as he had been before. We must, after all, be sensible.

This objection, right though it may be in the external sense, is opposed to everything we bear within us, first as concept and then as living Anthroposophy, that has to do with the working of the supersensible world and the passage over the threshold. It is an objection that has arisen out of the paradox of materialism.

Let us therefore mention in a few words two other *mysticisms* which belong to the foundations of anthroposophical thinking. One has been mentioned already in Rudolf Steiner's answer to the objection raised during the Christmas Conference that the *Goetheanum* no longer existed: *The Goetheanum* is still here — it is only the Building we have lost! The second is described as a *mystical fact:* The death on Golgotha and the appearance of the Christ in the etheric world.

This is the Mystery of the age in which we live: The next step mankind has to take is to rise above the materialistic, physical, earthly world of the senses and press forward into the reality of the supersensible, etheric world. Herein lie the mighty future events and life of mankind. After death, an ordinary mortal sees his etheric body depart from him and dissolve into the etheric universe. But this does not happen with the specially-formed, wisdom-filled etheric body of an initiate. This means, quite literally, that after his *death* Rudolf Steiner's etheric body remained and works on in a spiritual form in a way which is perhaps unique to him. "The etheric body and the astral body, if they are purified through and through and spiritualized, do not dissolve after death."[57] We should see in all this an urgent need for development and spiritual education in the Anthroposophical Society so that we may start to work in earnest on what is called etheric clairvoyance. Rudolf Steiner regarded the fact of an individuality working on in spirit as a reality, as may be seen in his lecture of 16 September 1924:

'And now if we would find a great helper for those things which we must investigate for the future of the 20th century, if we would find one who can advise us in relation to the supersensible world, if we need impulses that are there within the world, it is the individuality of Julian the Apostate — Tycho Brahe who can help us. He is not on the physical plane today; but in reality he is always there, always ready to give information on those matters especially which concern the prophetic future of the 20th century."[51]

Thus, after laying down his physical body, Rudolf Steiner too, with regard to his higher powers, was capable to a far greater degree even than before of remaining united with the service of Michael and with the Anthroposophical Movement. The Society, as the vessel for Anthroposophy and as the bearer of the esoteric, spiritual impulses of the Christmas Conference, is the body with which Rudolf Steiner remains united in order to work at his spiritual task.

The words he spoke after the death of Sophie Stinde will remain for us an unforgettable pointer on our path: "Those of us who truly and honestly acknowledge the spiritual world may count those who have merely altered the form of their existence but who remain faithfully united with us as souls, even though they have passed through the portal of death, among our most important and meaningful co-workers . . . Let us thank our dead friends for remaining among us so that in unity with their forces we may carry on our obligation to work for the spiritual culture of the world."[52] In this sense we may accept the fact of Rudolf Steiner's continued work "among us" as a reality.

In the 20th century the Etheric Christ is moving amongst mankind. And He is accompanied by one who placed into our world the Christmas Conference in the spirit of the Christos-Sun as the Beginning of a New Cosmic Age.

The Foundation Stone Meditation

Intimate reflection on the Foundation Stone Meditation brings us directly to the essence of the Christmas Conference. F.W. Zeylmans van Emmichoven[59] has elaborated a superb commentary on these Verses, opening for many members the way to their spirit light. In particular he has revealed the spiritual context of the rhythms and thus given insight into their lofty meaning.

Another aspect to be discovered is the revelation to be found in the Foundation Stone Meditation of a definite step forward taken by the human being. This would mean that it should be possible to show what could be described as an entirely new basis for the nature of man on which rests the existence of mankind.

Rudolf Steiner explained the beginning of the Meditation by saying that the human soul is calling out to itself. It is summoning itself to develop self-knowledge. In this way the Meditation establishes continuity with the working of the Mysteries from the distant past of mankind which were always expressed in the words *Know Thyself.* From the very beginning of earth evolution there has lived in the human soul the deeply grounded urge to incarnate in a body. Under the most varied conditions this impulse has had to find its way from earliest times up to the present day and it will continue to do so far into the future. Through this effort, forces are developed which will enable the human being to cope rightly with his task on earth. In the past, support was given by spiritual beings. Now, in the new Mystery Age in which we live, this process of incarnation is coming to the conscious knowledge of the human being.

The Foundation Stone Meditation begins with the soul calling out to itself its threefold links with its bodily sheath. The soul must learn to recognize quite consciously that the way into incarnation in a body lies *from below upwards.* In the same way when the human being wakes up in the morning the astral body and the ego enter in at the limbs and work their way through to the head. Proceeding step by step from the *limbs* to the *heart and lung organization* and finally to the *region of the head,* the soul finds the spheres in which it lives and through which it is to experience the mystery of man and the cosmos. This mystery speaks to the soul in the way the verses travel upwards from below:

Soul of Man! Thou livest *in* the limbs.	Soul of Man! Thou livest *in* the beat of heart and lungs.	Soul of Man! Thou livest *in* the resting head.

The great mystery which the soul is to learn through the limbs is the relationship between the limbs with their movements and the spirit. For the human body is spirit through and through. In a course of lectures Rudolf Steiner threw entirely new light on this fact: "Both matter and spirit are founded on something higher. And we can say: When this higher element is brought to rest, then it is matter; and when this higher element is caused to move, then it is spirit."[60]

By applying this truth to the method of teaching, he imparts to the teachers a comprehensive knowledge of man: "When the child does eurythmy he is brought into movement and during the course of this movement the spiritual element in the limbs streams upwards from the organs. When the child makes eurythmy movements or sings, the spirit is released. The spirit that is teeming in the limbs is released."[60]

We see here a living sea of spirit surrounding the moving limbs. And within this abundance of spirit work the laws that permeate all the deeds and paths of man, the laws of destiny. For karma is one of the attributes of the will. It is a streaming of the supersensible, forming and revealing destiny, a part of the endless sea of spirit. All this would slip away into the sub-conscious if man were not to develop an exercise of soul which could act as a hold on this streaming and become a guide for the eye of the soul into the history of man's creation. The faculty to be developed is described as *recollection*. In the *Leading Thoughts* we find the following paragraph in the essay *What is revealed when we look back into repeated earth lives:*

"Now just as in his present earthly life man bears his experiences within him in the shape of memory, so does he bear within him as a cosmic memory all that he has undergone in the way above described. What is the earthly life of the soul? It is the world of our memories, ready at every moment to have fresh perceptions. In this interplay of memory and fresh experience, man lives his inner life on earth. But this inner life on earth could not unfold at all if there were not present still in man, as a cosmic memory, what we see when we look back with spiritual vision into the first stage of his becoming earthly man — the stage in which he has not yet detached from divine-spiritual being."[61]

This quotation will have to suffice as an indication of the links between the power of recollection and the finding of the World-Creator-Being where one's own I is still embraced in the I of God from which it is just beginning to break away and come into being on its own account.

This Meditation can now live and resound in quietness of soul on the basis of a knowledge of man; it is best experienced when spoken aloud:

"Soul of Man!
Thou livest in the limbs
Which bear thee through the World of Space
Into the ocean-being of the Spirit!
Practise Spirit-Recollection
In depths of Soul
Where in the power sublime
Of World-Creator-Being
Thine own I
Comes to full being
In the I of God:
And thou wilt truly *live*
In Human-Cosmic-Being."

In its threefold form the Foundation Stone Meditation bears witness to the fact that man is a being of cosmic spirit, a being of soul and a being of spirit and body; and that he is embedded in the macrocosm and also linked to the hierarchies and also develops forces for the future. New processes of soul start to work within him when he carries out the three exercises of Spirit-Recollection, of Spirit-Meditation, of Spirit-Vision. The Meditation tells us exactly whither the soul is led when it immerses itself utterly in the verses.

The focal point of the Foundation Stone Meditation is knowledge of the I. This is contained in the threefold nature of the verses in such a way that it takes on the character of an initiation of the I. From beyond the threshold the immortal being of man sees what connects the ego-nature of man with initiation. The being of man lives in this initiation impulse in accordance with its spiritual origin if it accompanies the incarnation of the soul into the body from a supersensible standpoint. Only from beyond the threshold does the human being appear as a threefold form built in accordance with the secret of the I. It is this secret to which the Foundation Stone Meditation leads us. The system of the limbs, the system of the heart and lungs and the system of the head and senses are forms which show us the cosmic background of the evolution of the I. Thus we have to pass through three stages of ego-evolution on the path of incarnation; this accompanies the life of every individual like a biographical initiation theme. The effect of the Foundation Stone Verses is revealed particularly clearly in the way in which they raise consciousness of the ego's path through life. And the ego-character of the four-line rhythms reveals the new path given to us in the Christmas Conference:

Practise	Practise	Practise
Spirit-Recollection;	Spirit-Meditation;	Spirit-Vision;
Thine own I	Thine own I	To thine own I
Comes to full being	Unite	Grant
In the I of God.	With the Cosmic I.	For freedom of the will.

We can see in this the spiritual path of the soul to its higher ego, to the Spirit-Self which even now is beginning to work in the consciousness soul.

In his often only brief indications about these rhythms, Rudolf Steiner described what is contained in such a rhythm as a "soul process" or "a statement about the cosmic secrets in so far as these cosmic secrets are resurrected in the human soul as human self-knowledge". These words provide spiritual guidelines for penetrating into the inner meaning of the verses. Once we realize that a "soul process" of this kind has to do with the development of the I, it becomes obvious that the totality of the verse is rooted in the divine-cosmic world and leads us to the "Human-Spirit-Depths". By imagining quite concretely the process of creation — "Thine own I comes to full being in the I of God" — we place ourselves in the midst of a cosmic mystery. When spiritual truths such as those contained in the Foundation Stone Meditation pass before our soul ever and again they bring about a substantial deepening of understanding. In connection with *Spirit-Recollection* we bring about as a special activity *the* soul process:

"And thou wilt truly live
In Human-Cosmic-Being."

The consequence of this inner process is a new uniting of the human being with the cosmos, through which he "*will* truly *live*".

The description *Human-Cosmic-Being* — the human being as cosmic being; the cosmic being as human being — which appears in the first verse and depicts an intimate mutual permeation of man and cosmos, and also the expression *wilt truly live* which belongs to it, both share a future orientation: "thou *wilt* truly live in Human-Cosmic-Being". We must come to understand that life on earth had been no longer *true,* it had no longer corresponded to the archetypal image of man. The link with the "Human-Cosmic-Being" was broken because the human being as a truly spiritual being could no longer fulfill what had originally been required of him. This far-reaching disturbance which had attacked the very root of his existence points to the events of what we call the Fall of Man. The archetypal image of man, which had arisen throughout aeons of time from Saturn, Sun, Moon right up to the beginning of Earth evolution, had become corrupted. If the Fall had not taken place man would have had a quite different physical body and a quite different life on earth. "At the beginning of earth evolution man would have been invisible, even in his physical body"[62] Rudolf Steiner concluded.

The luciferic attack known as the seduction of man damaged the spiritual laws of the archetypal image. The life of mankind no longer bore the characteristics of "truth". Let us remember once more the laying of the Foundation Stone of the Goetheanum Building when Rudolf Steiner gave an understanding of what had once been truth in the Mysteries by proclaiming the cosmic Our Father, the Universal Prayer:

> "The Evils hold sway,
> Witness of Egoity becoming free,
> Selfhood-Guilt through others incurred . . ."

Now at the Christmas Conference we have before us once again the laying of a Foundation Stone. We hear proclamations, new concepts which bear the character of a new archetypal image. They are, for instance, *truly live* and *Human-Cosmic-Being*. The cosmos of man's true becoming stands before us, united with the Father-God from whom a new image of man arises. The Christmas Conference brought us a new *Cosmic Prayer* containing proclamations which signify in their totality a revelation of the Christ Being working in our time.

To understand this reality we need to refer to the background knowledge given in 1911 by Rudolf Steiner in his lectures *From Jesus to Christ*. Here he introduced his audience to the working of Christ Jesus. By taking hold of a human body at the Baptism in the Jordan, the Christ, a god in an earthly body, was able to protect the physical, etheric and astral bodies, which had become his sheaths, from further attacks by the two great tempters, Lucifer and Ahriman. During the three years of his work on earth the three sheaths were transformed by the Christ Being, and this included, *as a new creation, the restoration of the original physical body* in accordance with the divine archetypal image that had existed before the Fall. At the death on the cross, when the earthly substance of the body crumbled away, the new *earthly body,* now the Spirit Body of the Christ, was born. Rudolf Steiner called this the incorruptible *phantom.* No powers of temptation lived in this phantom. As spirit Body it became from then on the *true body* of man. It entered once more into the cosmic laws appropriate to it and became again the *"Human-Cosmic-Being",* an invisible and immortal bodily form created as an archetypal image by the highest hierarchies. Rudolf Steiner said about this:

"It came to pass that this one man, who was the bearer of the Christ, had gone through such a death that after three days the specifically mortal part of the physical body hard to disappear, and out of the grave there rose the body which is the force-bearer of the physical, material parts. The body that was really intended for man by the Rulers of Saturn, Sun and Moon — the pure Phantom of the physical body . . . this it was that rose out of the grave . . . So are the spiritual bodies, the Phantoms for all men, descended from that which rose out of the grave. And it is possible to establish a relationship with Christ through which an earthly human being can bring into his otherwise decaying physical body this Phantom which rose out of the grave of Golgotha."[62]

In view of this new fact of creation that was brought into being for mankind through the Mystery of Golgotha, it can be expected that the new *Cosmic Prayer,* too, will give expression to this new Mystery of man's creation which will in the future more and more strongly determine and shape mankind. There is indeed such a passage in the first verse of the *Foundation Stone World Prayer* expressing this in the simplicity with which only the greatest truths can be stated:

"Practise Spirit-Recollection
In depths of Soul,
Where in the power sublime
Of World-Creator-Being
Thine own I
Comes to full being
In the I of God;
And thou wilt truly live
In Human-Cosmic-Being."

On the basis of this archetypal statement in the Foundation Stone Meditation we may perceive that a further consequence of the restored human body or *phantom* will be a complete transformation of man's soul life: Through this new, uncorrupted body man's ego will be enabled to find itself; man will rise to a clear, spiritual consciousness of the I. We may read about this in the seventh lecture in the cycle *From Jesus to Christ:* "If we had the complete physical body, as was intended at the beginning of the earth-existence, our soul-powers would reflect themselves in quite another way: we should then know in truth what we are. As things now stand, we do not know what we are because the physical body is not given us in its completeness."[62] And later:

"And we cannot comprehend Christianity unless we understand that at the time when the Events of Palestine were taking place, the human race on earth had reached a stage where the decadence of the physical body was at its peak, and where, because of this, the whole evolution of mankind was threatened with the danger that the ego-consciousness — the specific achievement of the earth-evolution — would be lost . . . The destructive element would have penetrated ever more deeply into the human bodily organism, and men born after the time when the events of Palestine were due would have had to live with an ever-duller feeling of the ego . . . But there came the Event of Golgotha, an Event which completely restored the lost principles of human evolution. In so far as man takes into himself . . . that which we have called the 'incorruptible body' . . . he will become more and more clearly aware of his Ego-consciousness, and of that part of his nature which journeys on from one incarnation to another."[62]

All these descriptions, taken together with what was given during the Christmas Conference, help us to see the *rhythms of the Christmas Conference* in all their great spiritual significance for the universe and man. Particularly in those verses which deal with the links between the I and the beings of the Trinity there stands revealed the restoration of the new spirit body. The verses reveal this spirit body as the bearer of the archetypal image restored through Christ. We can understand why such an entirely different and new soul life of man is beginning to emerge, a soul life that is waiting to be taught esoterically about the Anthropos, the being of man. Everything points to the Turning Point Of Time for mankind when living, feeling and thinking will once again be *true*.

With new consideration and understanding let us turn once more to the *Verses of Truth:*

Father-God
Practise Spirit-Recollection;
Thine own I
Comes to full being
In the I of God;
And thou wilt *truly live*
In Human-Cosmic-Being.

Son-God
Practise Spirit-Meditation;
Unite
Thine Own I
With the Cosmic I;
And thou wilt *truly feel*
In Human-Soul-Activity.

Spirit-God
Practise Spirit-Vision;
Grant
To thine own I
For freedom of the Will;
And thou wilt *truly think*
In Human-Spirit-Depths.

To conclude this contemplation of the Christmas Conference, let us briefly gather together our findings:

When we see and feel and live the substance of the Foundation Stone Meditation it becomes illumined by the event of the Christmas Conference. We actually begin to approach the true source, coming to understand the Christmas Conference as a real Beginning Of A Turning Point Of Time.

The Foundation Stone Verses contain Anthroposophy with its new orientation towards the I. And this is the language in which the Christ speaks to us today.

The Anthroposophical Society is based on this:

It is its Foundation Stone!

Notes

1 R. Steiner: Die Weihnachtstagung zur Begründung der Allgemeinen Anthroposophischen Gesellschaft 1923/24. Rudolf Steiner Verlag, Dornach 1963. Bibl. 260.

2 R. Steiner: Die Konstitution der Allgemeinen Anthroposophischen Gesellschaft 1923/24. Rudolf Steiner Verlag, Dornach 1966. Bibl. 260a.

3 R. Steiner: An Autobiography. Rudolf Steiner Publications, Blauvelt, N.Y. 1977. Bibl. 28.

4 R. Steiner: The Philosophy of Freedom. Anthroposophic Press, N.Y. 1964, Rudolf Steiner Press, London. Bibl. 4.

5 R. Steiner: An Outline of Occult Science. Anthroposophic Press, N.Y. 1972, Rudolf Steiner Press, London. Bibl. 13.

6 R. Steiner: Riddles of Philosophy. Anthroposophic Press, N.Y. 1973. Bibl. 18.

7 R. Steiner and Ita Wegman: Fundamentals of Therapy. Rudolf Steiner Press, London 1967, Bibl. 27.

8 R. Steiner: Knowledge of the Higher Worlds and its Attainment. Anthroposophic Press, N.Y. 1983, Rudolf Steiner Press, London. Bibl. 10.

9 R. Steiner: Guidance in Esoteric Training. Rudolf Steiner Press, London 1972. Bibl. 245.

10 R. Steiner: Schicksalszeichen auf dem Entwicklungswege der Anthroposophischen Gesellschaft. Philosophisch-Anthroposophischer Verlag, Dornach 1943.

11 R. Steiner: The Fifth Gospel. Rudolf Steiner Press, London 1968. Bibl. 148.

12 R. Steiner: The Gospel of St. Luke. Rudolf Steiner Press, London 1965. Bibl. 114.

13 R. Steiner: The Gospel of St. Matthew. Rudolf Steiner Press, London 1965. Bibl. 123.

14 N. Grosheintz-Laval: Erinnerungen im Gedenken an die Feier der Grundsteinlegung zum ersten Goetheanum am 20. September 1913. In "Mitteilungen aus der Anthroposophischen Arbeit in Deutschland", No. 25, Michaelmas, Stuttgart 1953.

15 F. Edelmann, Reinach (bei Basel), unpublished.

16 H. Muller: Spuren auf dem Weg. Mellinger Verlag, Stuttgart 1976.

17 R. Steiner: Der Entstehungsmoment der Naturwissenschaft in der Weltgeschichte und ihre seitherige Entwicklung. Rudolf Steiner Verlag, Dornach 1977. Bibl. 326.

18 A. Steffen: Meetings with Rudolf Steiner. Verlag für Schöne Wissenschaften, Dornach 1961.

19 I. Wegman: An die Freunde. Natura Verlag, Arlesheim 1968.

20 R. Steiner and M. Steiner von Sivers: Briefwechsel und Dokumente (1901-1925). Rudolf Steiner Verlag, Dornach 1967. Bibl. 262.

21 R. Steiner: Wahrspruchworte. Rudolf Steiner Verlag, Dornach 1978. Bibl. 40.

22 R. Steiner: Awakening to Community, Anthroposophic Press, N.Y. 1974. Bibl. 257.

23 R. Steiner: Ansprache an die Mitglieder vom 12. September 1920.

24 R. Steiner: Der Goetheanum-Gedanke inmitten der Kulturkrisis der Gegenwart. Rudolf Steiner Verlag, Dornach 1961. Bibl. 36.

25 R. Steiner: Knowledge and Initiation. Cognition of the Christ. Steiner Book Centre, Vancouver 1983. Bibl. 211.

26 R. Steiner: Der Baugedanke des Goetheanum. Verlag Freies Geistesleben, Stuttgart 1958.

27 R. Steiner: Karmic Relationships, Vol II, Rudolf Steiner Press, London. Bibl. 236.

28 R. Steiner: Die gesunde Entwickelung des Leiblich-Physischen als Grundlage der freien Entfaltung des Seelisch-Geistigen. Rudolf Steiner Verlag, Dornach 1978. Bibl. 303.

29 At the founding of the Anthroposophical Society in February 1913 after the separation from the Theosophical Society.

30 R. Steiner: Karmic Relationships, Vol V, Rudolf Steiner Press, London. Bibl. 239.

31 R. Steiner: Die menschliche Seele in ihrem Zusammenhang mit göttlich-geistigen Individualitaten. Die Verinnerlichung der Jahresfeste. Rudolf Steiner Verlag, Dornach 1966. Bibl. 224.
32 R. Steiner: Karmic Relationships, Vol. VIII. Rudolf Steiner Press, London 1975. Bibl. 240.
33 R. Steiner: Unsere Toten. Rudolf Steiner Verlag, Dornach 1963. Bibl. 256.
34 H. Jenny: Morde, Brande, Skandale. Ein Panoptikum aus Basels finsterster Geschichte. Basler Schriften, Vol. 18, Pharos Verlag, Basel 1970.
35 M. Steiner: Vorwort zu R. Steiner, Die Weihnachtstagung zur Begründung der Anthroposophischen Gesellschaft 1923/24. Rudolf Steiner Verlag, Dornach 1963. Bibl. 260.
36 R. Steiner: The Essentials of Education, Rudolf Steiner Press, London. Bibl. 308.
37 R. Steiner: The Easter Festival in relation to the Mysteries. Rudolf Steiner Press, London 1968. Bibl. 233.
38 R. Steiner: Mystyer Knowledge and Mystery Centres. Rudolf Steiner Press, London 1973. Bibl. 232.
39 R. Steiner: Mysterienstätten des Mittelalters. Rudolf Steiner Verlag, Dornach 1980. Bibl. 233a.
39A R. Steiner: Karmic Relationships, Vol. VI. Rudolf Steiner Press, London, 1971. Bibl. 240.
40 Francis Bacon of Verulam (22.1.1561-2.4.1626).
41 R. Steiner: Building Stones for an Understanding of the Mystery of Golgotha. Rudolf Steiner Press, London 1972. Bibl. 175.
42 E. Bock: Beiträge zur Geistesgeschichte der Menschheit. Vol 1, 2 and 3, Verlag Urachhaus, Stuttgart 1978.
43 R. Steiner: Karmic Relationships, Vol. III, Rudolf Steiner Press, London 1977. Bibl. 237.
44 R. Steiner: The Four Sacrifices of Christ. Anthroposophic Press, N.Y. 1981. Bibl. 152.
45 R. Steiner: Die Sendung Michaels. Rudolf Steiner Verlag, Dornach 1977. Bibl. 194.

46 R. Steiner: Mitteleuropa zwischen Ost und West. Rudolf Steiner Verlag, Dornach 1971. Bibl. 174a.
47 R. Steiner: Die spirituellen Hintergründe der ausseren Welt. Rudolf Steiner Verlag, Dornach 1977. Bibl. 177.
48 R. Steiner: Der Zusammenhang des Menschen mit der elementarischen Welt. Das russische Volkstum. Rudolf Steiner Verlag, Dornach 1980. Bibl. 158.
49 R. Steiner: Goethe as Founder of a new Science of Aeshtetics.
50 R. Steiner: The Redemption of Thinking,. Anthroposophic Press, N.Y. 1981. Bibl. 74.
51 R. Steiner: Karmic Relationships, Vol. IV. Rudolf Steiner Press, London 1983. Bibl. 238.
52 R. Steiner: Occult History. Rudolf Steiner Press, London 1982. Bibl. 126.
53 R. Steiner: World History in the light of Anthroposophy. Rudolf Steiner Press, London 1977. Bibl. 233.
54 I. Wegman: Essay dated 28 June 1925 in "Nachrichtenblatt 1925", Dornach.
55 Statutes of the Anthroposophical Society.
56 R. Steiner: Hochgradmaurerei. Lecture given 16 December 1904.
57 R. Steiner: Das Prinzip der spirituellen Ökonomie. Rudolf Steiner Verlag, Dornach 1979. Bibl. 109/111.
58 R. Steiner: Menschenschicksale und Völkerschicksale. Schicksalsbildung und Leben nach dem Tode. Rudolf Steiner Verlag, Dornach 1960. Bibl. 157.
59 F. W. Zeylmans van Emmichoven: The Foundation Stone. Rudolf Steiner Press, London 1963.
60 R. Steiner: Menschenerkenntnis und Unterrichtsgestaltung. Rudolf Steiner Verlag, Dornach 1978. Bibl. 302
61 R. Steiner: Anthroposophical Leading Thoughts. Rudolf Steiner Press, London 1973. Bibl. 26.
62 R. Steiner: From Jesus to Christ. Rudolf Steiner Press, London 1973. Bibl. 131.

63 R. Steiner: Karmic Relationships, Vol. VI, Rudolf Steiner Press, London, Bibl. 240.
64 R. Steiner: Last Address. Rudolf Steiner Press, London, 1967. Bibl. 238.